Kingston Presbyterian Church

Seventy five years : anniversary proceedings of the founding of the Presbyterian Church, Kingston, Indiana, held in the church edifice, December 17th and 18th, 1898

Kingston Presbyterian Church

Seventy five years : anniversary proceedings of the founding of the Presbyterian Church, Kingston, Indiana, held in the church edifice, December 17th and 18th, 1898

ISBN/EAN: 9783337305048

Printed in Europe, USA, Canada, Australia, Japan

Cover: Foto ©Lupo / pixelio.de

More available books at **www.hansebooks.com**

SEVENTY-FIVE YEARS.

ANNIVERSARY PROCEEDINGS

OF THE

FOUNDING

OF THE

PRESBYTERIAN CHURCH

KINGSTON, INDIANA

HELD IN THE CHURCH EDIFICE

DECEMBER 17TH AND 18TH, 1898

ALSO PORTRAITS OF FORMER AND PRESENT PASTORS;
EXTERIOR AND INTERIOR VIEWS OF THE
CHURCH EDIFICE, ETC.

INDIANAPOLIS
INDIANAPOLIS PRINTING CO.
1899

INTRODUCTION.

Jubilee exercises commemorative of the seventy-fifth anniversary of the founding of Kingston Church were held in the Kingston Presbyterian Church December 17th and 18th, 1898 Rev. Bartlett, pastor of the church, presiding, ex-ministers of the church present, Rev. Dr. Rankin, of Brigham, Utah, and Rev. Harry Nyce, of Peru, Ind. Exercises were opened by the singing of Coronation by the audience, followed by prayer by Dr. Rankin. After a short introductory talk by the Rev. Bartlett, the roll of the original members of the church was read from the old session book by J B. Hopkins, present clerk of the session ; Mr J. B. Robinson then spoke upon "The Fathers of the Church," and was followed by J. G. Donnell, whose subject was "The Early History of the Sabbath School." Mrs. M. C. Jensen then sang an alto solo, entitled "The New Kingdom," after which Dr. Rankin addressed the audience from the subject "My Thirty Years' Pastorate." Letters were then read by Rev. Bartlett from Rev. John C. King and Rev. H. M. Schockley, former pastors of the church ; also from Rev. G. D. Parker, Rev. Ben. Nyce, Mrs. N. H. Adams, Mrs. M. A. Hamilton and Mrs. Zerelda Lawson, after which an adjournment was taken and dinner served in the basement by the ladies of the church.

Promptly at 2:00 P. M the audience was called to order by Rev. Bartlett, and after a musical selection by the Clarksburg Presbyterian choir, extempore addresses were given by Revs. Van Buskirk, Parker and Murphy, of Greensburg, Rev. Stewart, of Spring Hill, and Rev. Adams, of St. Paul, Minn. This was followed by the history of the church by Miss Camilla Donnell. Mrs. Ada Stewart read a paper entitled "Our Preachers and Missionaries " After another selection by the Clarksburg choir, Rev. Bartlett read a paper entitled "The Church of To-day," and was followed by Rev. Harry Nyce, who delivered the concluding address, from the text "Thou Hast Kept the Good Wine Until Now."

The following pages record for the most part such exercises. With this brief introduction the Committee submits the work voluntarily assumed by it.

R. A. BARTLETT,
MISS CAMILLA DONNELL,
J. Q. DONNELL,
ORLANDO HAMILTON.

ANNIVERSARY EXERCISES.

SATURDAY, JANUARY 17, 1898.

At the opening of the exercises, 10:30 A. M., the auditorium was well filled. The interior of the church had been beautifully decorated by the Committee. An arch of holly and mistletoe, containing the words "Seventy-fifth Anniversary," was placed on the platform. Festoons of rare beauty were suspended. Pictures of two of the honored ancestors were placed on easels near the pulpit. Rev. R. A. Bartlett, pastor, conducted the opening exercises. After the opening song, the pastor spoke as follows :

" I wish to extend to all of you a very cordial welcome. While it is cold without, we trust you will not find our hearts cold. There is no ice in our greeting. Most gladly do we welcome you to this quiet country side, where for seventy-five years this church has stood, leading to Christ and blessing those who have passed through her doors. We are here to celebrate our seventy-fifth anniversary, and we ask you with heart and soul to do all you can to make the exerc:ses helpful to all.

" We are honored in having with us two of the former pastors of this church, who, by their presence and voice will do much to make this occasion enjoyable and uplifting.

" We cordially greet the former members of this church, and friends from neighboring churches. It is our desire not only to make this diamond jubilee a season of joy and feasting, but also a time of instruction and spiritual good to every one present. We want everyone to feel perfectly at home, and not be embarrassed because of the clergymen present. They are fallible creatures. I have some good jokes on all of them, but I haven't time to tell them. I will give this one on Brother Nyce. I heard he was persuaded once to buy some hogs. Preachers are sometimes led astray in this direction. As soon as they were driven into the barn yard he climbed up into the mow and threw down a lot of hay for them. The hogs simply smelled it ' Pshaw,' said the disgusted parson, ' these hogs won't eat anything ! '

" It is my desire that this shall be the time when we shall become more earnest in the cause of the Master. Perils surround us — drink, Mormonism, greed, the disturbed relations of capital and labor, and other things suggestive of dynamite and bombs. There has never been a louder call for a consecrated church than to-day. I want to greet the boys and girls, and tell them how glad I am to see them here. The hope of this church is in you. You are to take the places of your fathers and mothers soon We want you to enjoy yourselves and feel this is your church. As we all rejoice to-day, let us thank God, and take new courage for the future."

The roll-call of the original members of the church was read by J. B. Hopkins, clerk of session, and elicited great interest.

Mr. J. B. Robison then spoke on " Fathers of the Church." From Mr. Robison's extended knowledge of the original supporters of the church, he was able to make an interesting and forcible presentation of the subject. The people were led to see, perhaps as never before, how much they were indebted to the noble men of the past.

Then followed J. G. Donnell's address on " The Early History of the Sabbath School." His talk was well received and highly appreciated by the audience.

Mrs. Jensen sang very sweetly the solo, " The New Kingdom." ·

Dr. Rankin's address on " Thirty Years' Pastorate " followed. He said in part :

" From a thirty years' pastorate, I have learne l to value the individual church. It would be difficult to put too high an estimate upon the worth of this church in the community in which it has grown ; to the county ; to the State of Indiana ; to our country, and to the world.

" Few communities, if any, surpass this in those things that a Christian civilization and gospel thrift bring to men. ' Not slothful in business ' has been emphasized, with the fervent spirit, in serving the Lord. The vices of irreligion robbed other people of far more than the support of the church here has cost. And the contrast between this and many other places may be accounted for by the difference in the influence of the local church.

" The churches, as centers of influence promoting religion, morality and good citizenship, in Greensburg, Forest Hill, Union and Sardinia, reaching to the soutwestern corner of the county, and Clarksburg and Memorial to the northeastern corner, are the children and grandchildren of this organization. Granting all that other denominations have done, and thankful therefor, it still would be grand larceny to rob Decatur county of this chain of frugal thrift and Christian living that might well be portrayed upon the map by a band of light. It would be hard to conceive what would have been the condition of this county had the early settlers here not ' associated themselves together as a church.'

" They had learned to value the influence of the local church, and when the log meeting-house was raised to the square with the canopy of heaven for the roof, the black earth for the floor and the sleepers for pews, they sent Elder John McCoy to New Richmond, Ohio, to bring a pastor, Rev. Samuel G. Lowry, and his family. They arrived Saturday night, having made the journey in a two-horse farm wagon. Nevertheless, on Sunday he preached from the text ' Therefore came I unto you without gainsaying, as soon as I was sent for. I ask, therefore, for what intent ye have sent for me?' The history of the church answers the question. They sent for him for the good of the community, the country, the State, the county, and the world.

" I have spoken of the good to the community and county. But now, see the blessings that came to the State. In that log meeting-house Hanover College was organized, and the pastor of this church was a trustee ; from here they got Harrison Thomson, who filled a chair so many years in the faculty ; a daughter of this one whose picture is upon my left endowed a professorship to commemorate the name of her mother. The same, being a daughter-in-law to him whose picture is upon my right, finished and furnished Donnell chape' in memory of her husband. Your pastor was one of the trio that dedicated it, and this aged gentleman before me was present and gave them $1,000 in memory of the time when he and Harrison Thomson hoed corn together — barefoot boys.

"What would Indiana, or the United States, or the world have been without Hanover? And what would Hanover have been without Kingston?

"The most vivid imagination could not pictur · the condition of things to-day with these factors left out. Kingston furnished Bloomington a professor, and the Louisville Courier Journal its greatest editor. Your first pastor held the stake Carnahan drove to mark the place where Wabash College was built, and that Thomson who managed its finances so admirably for many years professed faith in Christ here. Rev. B. M. Nyce, another of your pastors, a born educator, laid the found it on for Professor Campbell's success Campbell was father of the centennial at Philadelphia in 1876, which was the forerunner of the great Chicago exposition and the lesser one at Omaha. How far-reaching the influence and how great the value of the church organized in a log cabin home seventy-five years ago! Can you think of Indiana without Wabash College as a factor in achieving her greatness, or our public schools without the formative work of Professor Mills?

"To measure the worth of this church, there must be a recalling of the Christian families gone to other parts of our land. You could start at Greater New York and travel to San Francisco and stop every night with one such.

"Her membership has gone beyond the oceans to the dark continent of Africa ; to Asia and to the islands of the sea. The joy of the whole earth was Mount Zion, and in entailing this church upon you younger people a goodly heritage is left for you to develop ; and as this beautiful building which is to be rededicated to-morrow surpasses any of the five churches built here before it, so it should be your Christian ambition to make the church worshiping within these walls surpass in beauty of holiness that which has preceded it. The church of seventy-five years to come should do more th n the church of seventy-five years gone."

After reading of some letters, extracts from which are given in this pamphlet, adjournment was made to the basement of the church, where dinner was served. Over 300 people sat down to the tables. Mrs. Chester Hamilton was chairman of the Entertainment Committee. The dinner was a bountiful one, tastefully served from prettily decorated tables. All the ladies doing their utmost to aid, made it a "royal feast" indeed.

At 2:00 o'clock the audience was called to order by the pastor. The Clarksburg Presbyterian choir sang a very beautiful selection. The pastor, in introducing the singers, stated they had never been known to quarrel. Rev. Van Buskirk, pastor of the Christian Church in Greensburg, arose to his feet and remarked that a picture of that choir ought to be made and placed in the souvenir pamphlet.

Extemporaneous addresses were then made by Revs. Van Buskirk, Parker and Murphy, of Greensburg ; Rev. Stewart, of Spring Hill, and Rev. Adams, of St. Paul, Minn. The spicy remarks of these brethren called forth rounds of applause.

REV. JOHN WEAVER.

Miss Camilla Donnell read an excellent paper,

HISTORY OF THE KINGSTON CHURCH.

"It was the wise and witty Dr. Oliver Wendell Holmes who said that 'To treat a disease in time, you must often go as far back as a man's grandfather.' So, to fully understand this church, we must trace it back to its origin in the old Concord church in Bourbon county, Kentucky. The ancestry of all the pioneer fathers of the church was practically the same. Of Scotch Irish descent, and therefore, as one of them quaintly says, 'Presbyterian as far back as we have any record.' They emigrated from western Pennsylvania to Kentucky with their parents from 1784 to 1790, where in 1792 they founded Concord Presbyterian church.

"In 1817 Rev. John Rankin, the noted divine and abolition leader, became their minister. He records that in this church of over 200 members, in a slave State, there was but one slave-holder. He found in it an active society for the abolition of slavery. Some of its more prominent members held meetings, circulated books and tracts against slavery, and so far as they had means, carried on suits in behalf of such slaves as were held contrary to law. Such a community could have no true home in a slave State. From 1821 to 1823 a number of families emigrated to the then new State of Indiana, and located in the bounds of what is now the Kings'on neighborhood. Our ancestors have left us few written memorials of those days. The little old session book, yellow with age, yet well preserved, and written for the most part in the clear, old-fashioned handwriting of Samuel Donnell, the first clerk of sesson, and kept with a methodical accuracy that might have served as a model for later generations, is the most interesting relic of that early period. The first record is dated simply December, 1823, leaving blank the name of the day of the week and month. The day we celebrate, December 18th, appears to have been fixed upon at the fiftieth anniversary, by the rather uncertain recollection of survivors. The place of meeting was near Carmel church, on a farm forming part of that now owned by Mrs. Wesley Throp. In the session book, the only contemporaneous record, it is described as the house of Samuel D. Henry, but was better remembered afterward as the home of his father, William Henry, one of the most honored elders of the old Concord church, but never a member of this church, he having died before its complete organization. The record proceeds, 'This day, agreeable to previous notice, a number of persons, who had formerly been members of the Presbyterian church, came forward after sermon by the Rev. John Moreland and associated themselves together as a Presbyterian church, to be denominated Sand Creek church, and proceeded to choose Samuel Donnell, John Hopkins, John C. McCoy and William O. Ross to the office of ruling elder.' Rev. John Moreland, who organized the church, was a well known minister in Kentucky, and is still dimly remembered by some of the older people as afterward visiting and preaching to the church.

"Samuel Donnell and John Hopkins were both past middle life. Both had been leaders and ruling elders in the church in Kentucky. Both were for that time well educated and thoroughly versed in the doctrines of the church, and were able theologians. Both were men of unusual ability and force of character, and differing as they did on public questions, they afterward became leaders in opposite factions in the church. William O. Ross lived near Greensburg, and united with the church of that place on its organization. Uncle John McCoy survived all his first colleagues many years, and is still affectionately remembered by the present generation. No other minister seems to have visited the infant church until September 4th and 5th of the following year, 1824. Rev. John Dickey, an able pioneer preacher well remembered and greatly beloved by all the older people, held a two-days' meeting at the home of Cyrus Hamilton. He ordained John McCoy and William O. Ross to the office of ruling elder, and installed Samuel Donnell and John Hopkins, who had been previously ordained. The session then held its first regular meeting, and the fifty persons whose names were read this morning, having, as the record says, 'presented letters or other satisfactory evidence of membership in other churches, were received as members of the Sand Creek church.' It is now seventeen years since the last survivor of these charter members, Mrs. Cyrus Hamilton, was laid to rest in the Kingston cemetery. Only two persons are living who were present and were old enough to have remembered this meeting, Mr. Marshall Hamilton, now eighty-seven, and Mrs. Minerva Donnell, nearly eighty-two. Of the young children who were carried there in the arms of their parents, six still survive — Robert A. Hamilton, William M. Hamilton, Orville Thomson, Mrs. Polly Ann Jones, Mrs. Margaret Miller and Mrs. Warder Hamilton. Of these eight survivors, five are descendants of Mrs. Mary Edward Hamilton. All of the eight are residents of this county, and all save Mrs Miller and Mrs. Hamilton are present at this meeting. Of the eleven children presented for baptism at this time, the following are familiar names : John Hopkins Donnell, Margaret Jane Donnell, Orion Wallace Donnell, Katy Jane Hopkins, Margaret Mitchell Hamilton, Harriet Newel Hamilton and Angelina Antrobus. On August 27th and 28th, 1825, nearly a year later, Father Dickey again visited the church, and again held a two-days' meeting at the home of Cyrus Hamilton.

"It is surely not amiss to offer a tribute to the early mothers of the church, who joyfully entertained the home missionary in their one and two-roomed cabins, cooked on their open fireplaces the best they could set before him, and opened their doors to the entire congregation for meeting. At this time the session received the first members on profession of their faith. They were Cyrus Hamilton, Samuel Hamilton, Benjamin Antrobus and Mrs. Martha Mars. Although preaching services were held but once a year, as we have seen, from 1823 to 1826, prayer-meeting and Bible examination by the elders was kept up on Sundays. On June 3d, 1826, Rev. S. G. Lowry visited and preached to the church, and at this meeting an order from Presbytery was read granting leave to a number of members, twelve in all, to be stricken off and organized into a church at Greensburg. August following the congregation met to choose a minister, and Rev. S. G. Lowry, who was already supplying the church, was duly chosen by unanimous vote, and was installed November 8th by Madison Presbytery.

"Rev. Mr. Lowry and his wife, Almira Lowry, who was a member of the Thomson family, were greatly beloved by the congregation, as the frequent recurrence of both their names on the baptismal register shows. It also suggests, taken with the meager salary he received, the explanation offered by one of these witty namesakes, that the people of those early days paid their preacher by naming their children after him. Mrs. Lowry died in 1828, and her grave was the first in the unfenced, new graveyard. In the summer and fall of 1828 Mr. Lowry had very successful revival meetings, and gathered into the church, besides the older persons received by letter, about thirty-five young people, who for many years were the pillars of the church. These are some of the familiar names : James Hamilton, Luther Donnell, John Thomson, John R. Donnell, Angus C. McCoy, Sally Hamilton, Alexander Thomson, Harvey Antrobus, Thomas Hamilton Antrobus, Marshall Hamilton, Jam s Ardery, Jane Braden, Samuel Addison Donnell, Polly Robison, John C. Donnell, Elisa Jane Hopkins, Elenor Hamilton, Olesa Donnell.

"John Hopkins and William O. Ross, having become members of the Greensburg church, an election was held September 26, 1829, to fill their places in the session. Thomas Hamilton, John Kirkpatrick and James A. Thomson were duly elected. Thomas Hamilton was at this time just thirty-one years old. He served the church as an elder fifty years, the longest service in the history of the church and one of rare benignity and honor. August 26, 1832, we find this record : ' On this day Rev. Samuel G. Lowry delivered his farewell address to this church and congregation.' Mr. Lowry lived to a green old age, and was present as the central and honored figure at the fiftieth and sixtieth anniversaries of the church, whose first pastor he had been.

"In April, 1833, Rev. John Weaver began his ministry in the church, and was installed the following year by the Presbytery of Indianapolis. Our fathers were more formal in this matter than their descendants, Messrs. Lowry and Weaver being the only ministers in the history of the church who were installed.

"Rev. Weaver seems to have been a man of considerable force of character, and if we may judge from the records, of a somewhat aggressive temper and a strict disciplinarian. During the first twelve years of its history, the records of the little church do not show a single case of discipline or of any charge preferred by brother against brother. But, about 1835 it entered upon a new and troubled page of its history. Session frequently admonished refractory members. Charges were often brought for trivial offenses, and frequent complaints of slander show that a great deal of heated and angry controversy was being indulged in. The student of these records soon becomes convinced that the church and even the session itself were being divided into two hostile and apparently irreconcilable parties. This was not the fault of any one man or set of men. It was simply that ' the irrepressible conflict,' afterward to convulse the whole nation, had at the little Sand Creek church already begun.

"September 24, 1836, Samuel Donnell laid before the session a paper ably reviewing and severely condemning the course of the General Assembly on the subject of slavery, concluding with the decl ration that so long as the church continues to give her countenance and support to the crying sin of oppression, she must expect the displeasure of God and the scorn of infidels to rest upon her, and resolving that the foregoing paper be sent up to Presbytery as an overture from this session, asking the opinion of Presbytery on the subjects therein contained. Whether this paper ever reached Presbytery or not does not appear ; but in November Presbytery held a two-days' session at Sand Creek, and directed that in view of the difficulties existing in the church a vote be taken by the congregation on the acceptability of the several members of session. December 22d this meeting was held at Thomas

Hamilton's house, the meeting-house we are told being uncomfortable, and Samuel Donnell and John C. McCoy were voted unacceptable and Thomas Hamilton, James Thomson and John Kirkpatrick were voted acceptable. Thomas Hamilton immediately resigned, and his resignation was accepted. At a subsequent meeting Joseph Graham, Sr., Robert Hamilton and James Ardery were elected to fill the vacancies thus occaisioned. The crisis had now been reached. On March 13, 1837, Thomas Hamilton laid before session a paper giving notice that the undersigned members of the Sand Creek church wish to withdraw and do withdraw their membership from said church. This paper was dated March 4, 1837, and was signed by thirty-seven members. All of these persons, with two exceptions, belonged to the three families of McCoy, Hamilton and Donnell and those connected with them by marriage, including in the family of Samuel Donnell, Andrew Robison, Jr., and Preston E. Hopkins.

" The seceding church, which grew into what is now the Kingston Presbyterian Church, was in a decided minority, the whole number of members before the division being given three years before, in 1834, at 167. All its records up to 1863, when a new session book was begun, have unfortunately been lost, so that for facts and dates up to that time the historian has had to depend upon a careful comparison of the recollections of the older members. The records of the older church have apparently suffered the same fate.

" The following dates in its history have been as carefully verified as possible under the circumstances. Rev. Joseph Monfort, so long the senior editor of the Herald and Presbyter, then a young man just beginning his career, succeeded Mr. Weaver in 1839. He was not only a minister of ability, but a man of great tact and good judgment. His influence doubtless did much to lessen the antagonisms caused by the division. It is a proof of the strong common sense and good feeling of both churches that no feuds grew out of the separation, and from this time until they were once more one church, with the exception of some natural jealousies, mutual respect and good feeling existed between them. Rev. Monfort was succeeded in 1841 by Rev. Adams, and he in turn by Rev. David Monfort, an uncle of Joseph Monfort. Mr. Monfort gave place to his son-in-law, Rev. John King, in 1844, who has perpetuated his memory among us by laying out and giving his name to the village of Kingston, and ultimately to the church. Mr. King still lives, at an advanced age, in Arkansas. Rev. William Stryker supplied the church from about 1852 to 1856. Rev. H. M. Shockley, who became minister about 1857, is remembered as an agreeable young man, of excellent social qualities and a favorite with young people Rev. Van Nuys was the last pastor, supplying the church during the first years of the war.

" While the new church, as we have seen, was composed of a few large families living around the village and gradually spreading out on adjoining farms, the members of the older church lived mainly on the borders of the community. Gradually it suffered the fate of many country churches. Some of its wealthy members connected with the Greensburg church. Some died, many removed to other places. Early in the sixties it had become so weakened that services were practically discontinued. In matters of doctrine and politics the two churches were now one, and its remaining members were about this time gradually absorbed into the sister church. To go back to the history of the seceding church, finding itself outside the Presbyterian fold, it sought a temporary shelter in the Congregational church. Its first minister after the division was Rev. M. H. Wilder, a Congregational minister living in Franklin county, who was engaged for one-fourth of his time, and remained a year. In 1840 the little frame church, which afterward served the community as a school-house, was built.

"Rev. Benjamin Nyce, afterward destined to fill a larger space in the church and neighborhood, was then principal of the Greensburg Seminary, and for two years supplied the church on Sundays.

"Rev. Charles Chamberlain, a young man from the East, succeeded Mr. Nyce, remaining about a year. He was popular with the congregation, and much deplored when he returned to the East, married a wife and therefore could not come back.

"The New School church had in 1838 broken off from the old, and the fathers, probably never much at home in Congregationalism, gladly united with it. Rev. Mr. Boram, formerly of the Episcopal church, and living in Greensburg, about this time supplied the church for a few months, and is only vaguely remembered. He was succeeded in 1842 by Rev. Mr. Campbell, who remained about a year. He was a preacher of ability, though of somewhat eccentric disposition.

"From about 1844 to 1847 Rev. Jonathan Cable supplied the church, and his wife kept a private school at their home. Mr. Cable was an energetic farmer as well as minister, and an earnest anti-slavery worker.

"Rev Benjamin Franklin, who came to the church in 1847, was an Englishman, fresh from missionary life in the West Indies. The church was now firmly established, and the community had become prosperous, and even wealthy. Nevertheless, the crude Western ways of living made a great impression on Mr. Franklin, especially the tobacco chewing, and he could give in after years some amusing reminiscences of those early days. He was a genial, cultivated gentleman, and with his excellent wife, was a great favorite with young and old. During his pastorate a separate church was organized at Clarksburg for the convenience of a number of members living near there. Luther Donnell was prominent in its organization, and was its first elder. In 1850 Rev. Benj. M. Nyce, who had become a son-in-law of the church by his marriage with Melissa Hamilton, again became its minister. Mr Nyce was a preacher of great originality and force. Both as a minister and principal of the school for a number of years, he left a lasting mark on the rising generation. During his ministry, in 1850 or 1851, the most radical element of the New School body seceded from it and formed the Free Presbyterian church, which excluded from its membership all slave-holders and made war on all secret societies. With this body, which of course represented the most extreme anti-slavery element, this church gladly united.

"We cannot resist the conviction that this worthy body of reformers con ained a good many cranks, and Kingston probably had its full share, both of preachers and members. But our fathers were happily unconscious of the word. They went on their way quite regardless of the ridicule or the prejudice of the outside world, with temperance and abolition written on their door-posts, reading and circulating abolition books and papers, attending distant anti-slavery conventions in their old-fashioned carriages, running with great success their branch of the underground railroad, voting the most extreme reform tickets and doing their humble best to turn the world up-side-down. Like all reformers, their zeal was not always according to discretion, but they left behind them a glorious record, the precious heritage of their children's children, down to the present generation.

"About 1854 Mr. Nyce resigned the church, and Rev. Daniel Gilmer became its preacher for the next three years. Mr. Gilmer was an able preacher and a forcible debater, and his interesting family of young people were a great social addition to the church. In 1857 the synod of the Free Church was held at Kingston, an occasion always much referred to. Among the more fervid orators was Rev. William Perkins, of Cincinnati. On the retirement of Mr. Gilmer, he was called to the church. He retained his home in the city, boarding round among the people a part of each week. He was a controversialist, a brilliant talker and a most persuasive borrower. No minister has preached to the church of whom so many good stories are told.

" In December, 1860, the church being once more vacant, Rev. A T. Rankin, son of Rev. John Rankin, of Ripley, entered upon his thirty years' pastorate. His ancestry, his early training, as well as his own personality, made him peculiarly acceptable to the Kingston people. Early in his ministry the church, as we have seen, became the one united church of the neighborhood, and entered on a career of growth and prosperity before unknown. It was during this period the parsonage was built, land was added to it, large bequests were received by the church from some of the noble pioneers who had done so much to build it up, a cemetery fund was raised, and finally the present modern building replaced the old frame church. In 1870 Dr. Rankin held the most successful revival meetings in the history of the church, out of which grew in the following year the organization of the Memorial church. It was during his pastorate that a large and successful Woman's Missionary Society was organized. It is this period over which the historian of the hundredth anniversary will linger with pride, where he will vainly explore for facts and figures the failing memories of the survivors of this occasion. It will be his province, not mine, to speak of the eminent services Dr Rankin has rendered this church and community, and to picture the respect and affection in which he was held during that long period by all the country around. During this period, also, the church has suffered its severest bereavements. All the pioneer fathers and mothers, save two, who had borne the burden and heat of the day for more than a half century, ' fell on sleep,' and were carried one after another from the old frame church and laid to rest in the cemetery across the road. They were a noble ancestry, of sterling intelligence, frugal in their lives, devoted to every reform, always rich toward God and the church. With all due respect for the present and all due hope for the future, we say, Kingston church will never look upon their like again.

From 1890 to 1892 Rev. J. A. Liggitt was pastor of this church. From August, 1892, to January, 1894, all too brief a time, Rev. Harry Nyce, son of Rev. Benjamin Nyce, was with us, and in October, 1894, Rev. R. A. Bartlett became our minister, and long may he go in and out before us. The events of these years are too recent to need recalling here. These brethren are all young men, and can well afford to wait until the hundredth anniversary to hear their eulogies from some more gifted pen. We trust they may come back to us from places of honor and influence to grace the occasion with their eloquence and their gray hairs and exchange reminiscences of this day with the well-preserved old gentlemen and old ladies who will still survive it. It will be for the chidren and young people of to-day to see that that anniversary finds here still strong and vigorous the church which their great grandfathers planted seventy-five years ago, amid so many hardships, and which their grandfathers and fathers have loved and tended till to-day.

"CAMILLA DONNELL."

Through mistake this well prepared paper of Mr. Everett Hamilton was not read until Sabbath.

OUR CHURCH EDIFICES—THE FINANCIAL RECORD.

"On anniversary occasions the one who indulges in anecdote and reminiscence may be allowed some latitude for the play of his fancy, and of incidents grown dimmer and dimmer by passing years, this latitude may widen and widen until it knows no bounds, but the one who writes history, if nothing else, must be truthful, and the story of transactions that have occurred and events that have happened beyond the memory of the living, should be verified by records that have been made and preserved.

"At the outset of this undertaking we are met with a difficulty in the scanty records to be found, for while those who have gone before us builded wisely and well, they kept no formal record of preliminary proceedings or financial outlays. The story then of the financial achievements of this church must consist of a simple narrative of its journey from the old log meeting house to the present edifice, as gleaned from the recollections of the living.

"There is, however, in an old session book, some records of church expenses and contributions to benevolence, which on account of their age may be interesting, and may also serve as a further introduction to this story.

"We copy from the old book:

" 'The following is here transcribed for the sake of preservation: On settlement with Robert B. Donnell and James Thomson, collectors for the Sand Creek congregation, the sum of $572.93¾ has been received in discharge of the pecuniary obligation of the call which I hold from said congregation up to the beginning of the year, January, 1829. The deficit of $27.06¼ is hereby relinquished to the credit of said congregation, so that this instrument shall be considered a clear receipt for three years up to January 1, 1829.

" 'Witness my hand this 9th day of January, 1830.

" 'SAMUEL G. LOWRY.'

"It is not an uncharitable reflection on the benevolence of the Rev. Samuel G Lowry, considering the meagerness of his salary, to credit the belief that probably the reason he relinquished the deficit was because the resources of the collectors were exhausted.

"This entry also appears:

" 'The following is transcribed for the same reason as above: Agreeable to the settlement this day made with the collectors of the Sand Creek church, I hereby acknowledge the receipt of $632.50 for the years 1829-1830-1831 and half of the year 1832.

" 'Signed August 25th, 1832.   " 'SAMUEL G. LOWRY.'

Rev. J. G. Monfort. D. D., LL. D.

"It will be seen from this that Mr. Lowry received for the years mentioned $180.87 per anumn, and that the services of a pastor, like other com-
modities of that period, were obtained at very reasonable rates.

"The entries in the old session book of the benevolent contributions for
the inspection of Presbytery are also interesting. From October, 1827, to
October, 1828, seventy-five cents were contributed to Presbytery; in 1828,
$3.00 for commissioners' fund; in 1830, $3.00 for commissioners' fund and
$10.00 for theological seminary; in 1831, $3.00 for commissioners' fund and
$40.00 for education.

"Having exhausted the old session book, let us consider for a little while
the log meeting house, which we are told was erected in 1826, and probably
stood on the highest point of ground directly west of the present edifice, in
the cemetery inclosure. We would very naturally picture this structure as
very crude, and to harmonize it with the cabins of the pioneers, would have
it built of round logs with a clap-board roof held fast by ridge poles, and so
generally finished as to let the weather in and keep the sunshine out, but we
are told by one who remembers it well, that in appearance it was respectable,
being built of poplar logs, nicely hewn with chinks well and neatly pointed.
We are also told that when it was no longer needed as a house of worship,
it was sold to John Hopkins, who it seems had a propensity for buying old
buildings and moving them on his farm. The transaction caused one of his
neighbors to remark that 'Uncle Jack's punishment in the next world would
be in seeing old buildings scattered around and that he would not be pre-
mitted to move them '

"The second edifice, erected in 1836, was a brick and stood to the north
in the same inclosure. The brick work was let William Walters, who lived
on a farm now owned by Henry Metz. The brick were made on his place
and hauled to the building site. The carpenter work went to a man named
Gerhart, and the two largest subscriptions for its construction were $50 00
each, given by Samuel and Jas. E. Hamilton. We are told by one who was
present, the way in which the contracts for this building were let, and it
seems so novel that it is worth recording. A day was appointed and the trustees and bidders were present, one of the trustees mounted a block and in auc-
tion fashion cried the bids, the rival bidders bidding back and forth, but of
course bidding down instead of up, finally the brick work was knocked
down at something like $500.00. In like manner the carpenter work was
let, but going at a smaller sum. Recollections of this edifice are vivid in the
minds of many. A long, low, roomy building with two entrance doors and
a high boxed pulpit between them; long narrow aisles and a low ceiling sup-
ported by many wooden posts, it also had many windows, but the brethren
who worshiped there did not all receive the same light, for we are told dis-
sensions arose and peace and brotherly love departed for a season.

"The third edifice, erected in 1840, was a frame and stood in the front of
what is now the schoolyard. This was not so large as the brick, but the
ceiling was higher and the windows larger, the entrance doors were double
—a middle aisle with the pulpit in the rear The failure to obtain any in-
formation as to the financial outlay incurred in the erection of this building
is complete. After twelve or more years of service as a house of worship, it
passed to the civil township and was used by the district school. The lumber for this edifice was sawed at a mill, whose power was furnished by a

large tread wheel on which cattle were worked, owned and operated by Cyrus Hamilton. An incident is related in connection with this lumber that caused great worry to two of the worthies of the church, namely, Uncle John McCoy and Samuel Donnell. It seems that they had especial charge of drying the lumber and by some accident or neglect the kiln was consumed by fire. Their distress at this disaster was very great and was only removed when new logs were cut and sawed to replace the kiln that was destroyed.

"Coming on to 1854, we find the fourth edifice in process of erection. During the raising of the frame of this edifice there was a crash of falling timber, caused by the carelessness of the builder, which seriously injured five or six persons, one or two of whom were maimed for life. We are told that the funds for this were raised by an assessment, and that the basis of the assessment was the taxable property listed to each member as found in the county records. We are also told that but very few objected or refused to pay the full amount of the assessment. With such a record as this, the spirit of justice and fairness that abided with that body of worshipers cannot be doubted. It is here we find a scrap of paper, headed "Church Money " This paper has two columns of figures, one of "Receipts" and one "Expended." The receipts show collections of assessments from fifteen members of the congregation living south of the church, and make a total of $1,028.34. The expended column shows payments during the year to D. Welsh of $803 24, and for bible and "trimings" $5.25. The acknowledgments of these payments are from David Welsh to R. A. Hamilton, trustee of the Free Presbyterian church. We can reasonably conclude that this represents only the settlement of one of the trustees. and as the territory mentioned would only cover about one-half of the taxable property which formed the basis of the assessment, by doubling these collections we come very near the cost of the edifice, which was something over $2,000.

"About this time the parsonage lot must have been acquired, although we have been unable to find any record of date or purchase price. The writer remembers it as the old Parvin residence, the house was a cheap frame, and Parvin had a little shop on the corner where he and his boys made boots and shoes during the week, and Parvin led the singing in the old brick church on Sundays. The shop served at one time as the village postoffice, and Parvin as postmaster. Later on the brick building which now stands was erected in front, with material from the old brick church, the old frame serving as rear apartments to the new building. We are told the cost of this was about $2,000.

"Coming on this way we find no records of expenses or improvements. They kept no books in those days, but in the times before the civil war the writer remembers some munificent offerings from the congregation worshiping in that Free Presbyterian church, when the cause was the advancement of human freedom. On December 25, 1869, seventeen acres of land adjoining the parsonage were conveyed to the trustees, at a cost of $1,300.

"A financial record of a church that does not show that at some time it found itself in debt, would hardly be credited; so to maintain our standing in this respect, we mention a note which was dated February 7, 1870, for $544 payable one day after date, to the pastor then in charge, bearing ten per cent. interest and duly stamped and signed by S. A. Donnell and Jesse G. Donnell, trustees. This note bears some credits of interests and some

REV. JOHN KING.

payments on the principal and a statement that on January 1, 1872, it was cancelled by a new note. The new note besides credits of interest is receipted in full December 25, 1875, from proceeds of a subscription paper.

" It was probably in the year 1875 that Mr. James E. Hamilton, with that far-seeing wisdom that was characteristic of the man, and with a desire to do something that would be of permanent benefit to the church he loved so well, gave the sum of $2,000 as an endowment, the income from which should go to the regular expenses of the church. This was followed later by gifts of $1,000 each for the same purpose from Miss Mary E. Hamilton, R. M. Hamilton and Mrs. Sally Donnell, swelling the sum to $5,000, which has since been increased $200 by added income while the church had no pastor. For these generous gifts the church will ever hold those who gave them in grateful remembrance.

" The time is nearing when we must part from this old edifice as a house of worship, which is so well remembered by everyone, for in 1882 it was determined to build a new one, and the present edifice is the result. The digression will be pardoned if we here follow it to the end, and to most of us who have passed the noon hour of the day of life, it will be with feelings like those we would have in parting for the last time with a very near and dear old friend. After twenty-nine years of service as a house of worship, this edifice whose walls had echoed the voices of so many reformers and noted revivalists, was used as a hall for debating clubs, political harangues and entertainments of all sorts, until in the spring of 1892 it was destroyed by fire.

" Returning, we have left us a certified copy of a subscription dated May 12, 1882. Its conditions bind the subscribers when $8,000 are subscribed. It contains 102 signatures, three of which are for $1,000 each, one for $600, two for $500 each, and others from $400 down. The footings show $9,006 subscribed. There is also a copy of a supplemental subscription containing twelve names, subscribing $543. A study of the names appended to these subscription confirms the suspicion already aroused, that besides the membership, old acquaintances, sons-in-law and wards of the church were visited and that but few escaped. With this total of $9,549, preparations were begun for the new edifice. In February, 1883, the title of the ground on which it stands was conveyed to the trustees at a cost of $500, and during the year the building was completed and dedicated to the worship of Almighty God. The completed building, with its furnishings, cost probably $2,000 more than the funds that were provided in the record we have shown ; but, with the help of the young people and the ladies of the church, who have always been faithful and helpful, and further aid from friends who had already given generously, the bills were all provided for.

" In a book that is filled to its last page, on the fly leaf we find the following : ' I, R. B. Whiteman, assumed the duties of treasurer of Kingston Presbyterian church February 5, 1882, by order of the acting Board of Deacons, at which time there was no money in the treasury, but a debt of $25.03 due to the following named parties and amounts.' Mr. Whiteman has left us very complete records of the regular expenses of the church, including contributions to the church boards and offerings in great variety which occurred during his ten years of service. Occasionally, faithful to its old habits, we find the church coming up with a deficit, but invariably a foot note follows with a statement that the debt is discharged by a special sub-cription.

"In 1890 a barn was built for the parsonage at a cost of $300, and in 1892 improvements were made to the parsonage at a cost of $700. Later on, repairs and improvements have been made to the present edifice, including those of the present year, costing $600, and since 1892 the treasurers' annual statements have shown a balance remaining in the treasury.

"This, imperfectly sketched, is the financial record of the church. The complete record of its contributions for houses of worship, works of charity and benevolence, and aid extended in response to almost every conceivable call, can never be shown; and, although its financial strength has been weakened by the changes of ownership in the community and the centralizing tendencies of the age, forces which are affecting and changing the life of society and menacing the existence of the country church in parts of our land to-day, it stands with its old garments thrown off and adorned with its new, in strength and in beauty, and the day of its passing does not yet appear."

Mrs. W. K. Stewart gave an interesting and spicy account of "Our Preachers and Missionaries."

OUR PREACHERS AND MISSIONARIES.

"A short account of the ministers and missionaries who have gone out from the old Sand Creek church during the past seventy-five years will show that the influence of this church has reached almost around the globe. Her representatives have been at work in Korea, Egypt and Liberia; from California to New York, and in nearly every State in the Union.

"The first ministers from this church were Harrison and Wallace Thomson, who attended Hanover College soon after its organization in the thirties Harrison was for many years a professor at Hanover, but afterward removed to California, where he died about ten years ago.

"A colored man named Thomas Ware was brought here by William Henry, educated and sent out by the Colonization Society to Liberia. He was not a minister, but some years ago a Rev. Ware, presumably a son of his, attended the Methodist General Conference as a delegate from Liberia; so that Thomas Ware may be called the first missionary of the church.

"However, the first real missionary connected with this church was Andrew Jack. He was baptized, according to the record, in 1832. He was one of the early missionaries to Africa, going out some time in the fifties. He was obliged to return on account of ill health, but took up the work at home, and was engaged in mission work in Indian Territory at the time of his death.

"John Harney was another minister, a professor at Bloomington, Ind., and the noted editor of the Louisville Courier when it opposed George D. Prentice. Samuel Hicks Parvin was connected with this church from 1846 to 1856, and is now located at Muscatine, Iowa. Other ministers are Austin Thomson, deceased, and Eberle Thomson, now at Ripley, O. They were both graduates of Hanover College. Theophilus Lowry is a son of the first pastor of this church. George D. Parker was an elder in this church and Sunday-school superintendent, and is now preaching at Converse, Ind., while his son is pastor of the Greensburg church. Thomas D. Bartholomew gradu-

REV. H. M. SHOCKLEY.

ated from Lane Seminary in 1869, and after a pastorate of more than twenty years in northern Ohio, Michigan and Lawrenceburg, Ind., died at his home on White Lake, Mich., March 11, 1897.

"As the Jews claimed the children's children to the third and fourth generation, so will we. Rev. Harry Nyce is a baptized member of this church, while Rev. Benjamin Nyce was a member of the church at Clarksburg. Rev. Harry Nyce is now at Peru, Ind., and Rev. Benjamin Nyce is at Lockport, N. Y. Rev. Edward Adams is a missionary in Korea. H. B. Hamilton, son of S. H. Hamilton, preached in Kansas a short time before his death ; and Emmet Robison, son of Samuel D. Robison, is preaching in St. Joseph, Mo. Rev. E. A. Allen, of Kokomo. Ind., studied for the ministry while a member of this church. There were two other colored ministers, Rev. Andrew Jackson Davis, and Peter Prim, who died before his studies were completed.

" While our church still clings a little to the Pauline theory that women must not preach, she is very glad to use them as missionaries. Of these, we have Mrs. Annie Adams Baird in Korea, and Mrs. Cap Hamilton Henry in Egypt. Misses Eva and Rose Rankin have both taught mission schools in Utah. Miss Jean Rankin served the Woman's Board of Home Missions in the industrial department of Washington College, Tenn., while Miss Hannah Evans did the same at Huntsville, Tenn., and Manchester. Ky.

"A list of the ministers is as follows : Harrison Thomson, Wallace Thomson, Andrew Jack, John Harney, S. H. Parvin, Austin Thomson, Eberle Thomson, Theophilis Lowry, Geo. D. Parker, T D. Bartholomew, E. A. Allen, Harry Nyce, Benjamin Nyce, Edward Adams, H. B. Hamilton, Emmet Robison, with three colored ministers, A. J. Davis, Thomas Ware and Peter Prim.

" The foreign missionaries are Thomas Ware, Andrew Jack, Edward Adams, Annie Adams Baird, Cap Hamilton Henry. The home missionaries are Eva Rankin, Rose Rankin, Jean Rankin, Hannah Evans.

" Some one has said that a preacher without a good wife is like a pair of shears with only one blade. If this be true, we in justice should mention those of this church who have made good ministers' wives. These are the names : Margaret Donnell Rankin, Almira Thomson Lowry, Melissa Hamilton Nyce, Cassandra Donnell Walker, Mary Wilson Hendryx, Lizzie Shelhorn Allen, Annie Adams Baird.

CHURCH OF TO-DAY.

Paper by Rev. R. A. Bartlett.

" I know you will appreciate the intention which I express to make these remarks brief. Brevity is the best thing in an address, next to brain. The speaker need not be deficient in the former, if he is in the latter. We hear much said to-day about the decadence of the country church. It has in many places only a nominal existence. Like the old mill by the stream, it has seen its best day. In other places the country church is in a precarious condition. There are a number of reasons for this.

" People tire of country life, and coveting the modern conveniences, social and religious attractions of the town, move there and settle for the rest of their lives. They do this, notwithstanding the fact that 'God made the country and man the town.' We country preachers do not envy our town and city pastors these sturdy, vigorous Christians ; but we are sometimes put to our wit's end to fill up the gap made in our membership. Town churches would soon become extinct were it not for country Christians. In country districts, too, where the population is sparse, the ravages of death are more keenly felt. The staunch paying member is removed by death, and it is difficult to fill his place with one like him.

"The Kingston Church in the last few years has lost by removals and deaths. Still, we have made some progress, and the church of to-day is united and harmonious. Our audiences every Sabbath are well maintained.

"The finances are efficiently managed, and all expenses of the church are paid monthly. In one week the people subscribed $450 toward church improvements. In addition to this, the furnace was moved and remodeled, the basement excavated and cemented, as you have seen it. All of this shows a commendable degree of activity, and reveals the fact that we are far from being decadent. We have one hundred and forty-two members on the roll. The Sabbath-school has an enrolled membership of one hundred. During the past four years, we have received sixty-nine members, raised for benevolences $1,835, and for congregational expenses $4,160. The women are organized into Home and Foreign Missionary Societies and are doing a good work for the Master.

"The Y. P. S. C. E. numbers forty active members, and the Junior Society twenty. The officers of the church are capable and faithful men, and have always co-operated with the pastor. We hear the complaint that the church in some places is manless. This is not true of the Kingston Church. We are blest with men who are willing to give their time and energies to the work of the Lord. During the progress of repairs, the men of this congregation gave cheerfully of their time and money to the work.

"What shall I say of the faithful women? Time would fail me if I should attempt to enumerate their virtues. They do not excel simply in the direction of providing a good dinner. One feels like endorsing the remark of the distinguished Adam Clark, that 'you could set down one woman as the equal of seven and one-half men.' There is doubtless much truth in this, even if his moral equation cannot be proven mathematically.

"Our choir, while it has lost by weddings and removals, has always co-operated with the pastor. While I do not wish to deny any member of the choir the sweet delights and joys of wedded life, I hope the next weddings will not invade that corner of the sanctuary.

"The church has as nice a company of young men and women as you will find anywhere. They are not of the simple kind, that make a specialty of frivolity in and out of the church. They are sensible and kind-hearted, and are ready to do their part to advance the interests of the church. In short, the church of to-day is full of hope, trusting in the Head of the church.

"Pray for us that we may be divinely guided, kept from strife, and filled with the spirit of the Lord of Life. A church of power is made up of lives in whom Christ is a living reality. On the three superb arches of the Milan Cathedral, these three inscriptions are written : 'All that which pleases is but for a moment ; all that which troubles is but for a moment ; only that

REV. B. M. NYCE.

is important which is eternal.' May the Christ who gave Himself for us help us as a church to believe with the whole heart 'only that is important which is eternal.' "

Rev. Harry Nyce, of Peru, then delivered the concluding address, from the text, "Thou Hast Kept the Good Wine Until Now." The sermon was a very inspiring one, and was delivered with great earnestness and power. It was listened to with rapt attention by a very large audience, filling the auditorium and gallery.

Benediction pronounced by Dr. Rankin.

THE SEVENTY-FIFTH ANNIVERSARY SERMON,

PREACHED BY THE

REV. A. T. RANKIN, D. D.,

SUNDAY MORNING, DECEMBER 18, 1898.

"Psalm 48: 13-14.

"To-day, December 18, 1898, marks the seventy-fifth anniversary of the organization of this church. Rev. John A. Moreland, a Presbyterian minister held in high esteem in Kentucky, a man deeply imbued with the spirit of his Divine Master, visited this vicinity and preached at the house of Mr. Henry on the farm now owned by Mrs. Wesley Thorp. After the sermon, the Presbyterians present associated themselves together in a church. This was the first Presbyterian church in the county, and so far as I can find out, the first *church* in the county. I believe it was the grandest thing the fathers did for this neighborhood ; and under God it has proved a blessing to the county and the State ; to our country and the world. With Clarksburg and Memorial to the northeast, and Greensburg, Forest Hill, Union and Sardinia to the southwest, the county map might be made with a band of light diagonally across it.

"Many members have gone with your greeting to other towns, and ministers reared here have preached in numerous other counties. One could travel from Greater New York to San Francisco and stop over every night with some former Kingston Christian family. And of your members, foreign missionaries have gone to western Africa, to Egypt and Korea, till your religious domain girths the world ; and like the British Empire, the sun never sets upon it. But these things were mentioned particularly in the papers and speeches yesterday, so I dismiss them to remark :

" 1st. That the time in the history of this church is the most interesting period in the past. No seventy-five years equal it. And nearly as much has been done for the world through the church as during all the preceding centuries of the Christian era. Applied science, practical invention, improved machinery, are the product of Christian thought, and are evidence of Christian civilization. Note the facilities for traveling and transporting products, as steamboats and steamships, railroad communications, mails, telegraphs and telephones, tools and implements for shop, factory, farm and home, by which one man or woman does the work of several.

"It was on the 18th of December, 1860, that I came to Decatur county, and thus, this day that marks the seventy-fifth anniversary of the church also numbers the thirty-eighth year of my work with and recollections of the church. You would judge from my text that I wished to speak chiefly of what has come to pass during these years. ' Walk about Zion, and go round about her ; tell the towers thereof. Mark ye well her bulwarks, consider her palaces, that ye may tell it to the generations following.'

" I remark secondly : They have been years full of great events. They are unparalleled. The true history of those times is stranger than fiction. Beginning with 1860, it is probable that since the birth of Christ no like part of a century has equaled it in the production of that which is wonderful. The events in history, the discoveries of science and the productions of art have been on such a magnificent scale that if I had proclaimed them when I got off the cars thirty-eight years ago to-day, instead of employing me as your pastor you would have thought of calling two esquires to send me to an insane asylum. Had I said prophetically what history tells the generation following the one that called me, who could have believed it ? I came to stay till the beginning and end of the Civil War ; and to see your members sign the muster roll on this communion table, and fight till the most gigantic rebellion ever known was put down ; the unity of the country decreed ; freedom given the slave ; the ballot put in the black man's hand, and the doors of the public schools opened to his children ; the fugitive slave law repealed, and the constitution of the United States amended as at present ; Fred Douglas, marshal of the District of Columbia ; B. K. Bruce, registrar of the U. S. Treasury ; former slaves elected to Congress, and the way opened for black men in the regular army to cover themselves with glory, as the 24th did on San Juan-hill.

"Who would have thought I came to stay till Russia set her serfs at liberty, and France became a republic, and Von Molke led the sturdy Germans to the conquest of Paris ; till a man can preach the gospel in Rome, China and Japan with greater safety than Wendell Phillips once spoke in Cincinnati ; till heathen governments send commissioners here to learn the secret of our strength, and students to gather the curriculum of our colleges. Morse had years before made electricity on land, ask from Washington and Baltimore, ' What hath God wrought?'' but who imagined that during my stay with you the first Atlantic cable pronounced a success should be grappled up and made, in competition with others, to tell us what Kitchener did on the Nile the day before, or Dewey in the Phillipines?

" While we had many railroads in 1860, we had none that reached across the continent. I buried one of your number in that beautiful cemetery over the way who drove from here to Council Bluffs and returned without crossing a railroad or hearing a whistle. Another drove to Oregon and back, and one sitting with you to-day drove 1,000 or 1,500 miles farther than that miraculous journey. I hear the Mormon elders tell of from Omaha to Salt Lake. Were my friend to lay aside the cares of farm life a few days, he could find rest and recreation in going in a few days over the same route that took months before.

"Again, who would have been believed had he foretold the improvements in facilities for farming? Compare the first reaper even with the great harvesters now drawn by three or five horses, doing the work of twenty men with sickles in the olden time. Then in planting time, I remember a few men who, after the ground had been marked both ways, could walk between two rows and drop them ready for the coverers. Now one man with two horses, sitting on a spring-seat planter, does the work of six men.

"Then who would have thought of speaking in a natural voice to a friend miles away and recognize the tones of answer as if the lips moved against the ear. What a time saver the telephone is to you farmers. You want to borrow a harrow, ring up your neighbor a mile away, tell him what you want and request him to bring it over. Then when you are done with it, have a pleasant chat with him and let him know that he can have it when he comes. So easy to save his coming twice. Then with your houses heated and lighted by natural gas, and water for all purposes pumped by the wind, you never hear on a hot day, 'bring a pail of water or an armful of stovewood, quick.' You turn a faucet for one and a thumb-screw for the other. Now, without stopping to go over in detail a long catalogue of improvements in other things, and the wonderful events of the Civil War, the more wonderful achievements in the war with Spain, the things done in the realms of politics, in morals and religion ; without stopping to count the millions given for benevolent purposes, it is safe to say no man would have believed the half already told, had I prophesied it on December 18, 1860, much less had he dreamed it December 18, 1823.

"I remark thirdly : Just as wonderful things have come to pass in this vicinity. Things as marvelous, as unexpected, as incredible, humanly speaking, have transpired in the development of the Kingston Church. Suppose, when Thomas Hamilton and Addison Donnell took me out to one side, after I had preached, in ten days, half the sermons I had written, and asked me if I would preach here and at Clarksburg to the only Free Presbyterian churches in Indiana for $600 a year and the use of that little parsonage, and when I answered yes, I had added, and will stay with you till you give me more than three times as much rather than do without preaching, and one of your number will give annually one-third as much as all offer ; till the three little churches come together as three globules of mercury into one, and the 'Free,' 'New School' and 'Old School' Presbyterians lose their prefixes and become Presbyterians together.

"As many came to us from the M. E. Church as from the Old School Presbyterian. Yes, I will live in that little parsonage till you build a two-story brick front for $2,000 and buy that seventeen and a half acres for $1,500 and put up that new barn ; till Memorial is gathered and you contribute over $2,500 to build a church for them; and Clarksburg repair their building and beautify the grounds at a cost of over $1,200, and gather $400 as a nucleus for a parsonage fund. Till that cemetery be endowed and made one of the most beautiful spots on earth, in which to bury our dead. And then till you purchased the principal corner lot in the town and erected this beautiful building, which has been renovated and we rededicate to-day to the worship of God. When it was first dedicated, having no need for ourselves, we took up $120 for church erection. It was so unprecedented a thing that the board sent us a blank to fill with the name of a life member. It was unanimously voted to put in the name of T. L. Donnell, one of the building committee.

"Then who would have thought I would have stayed till four of your number would furnish $5,000 cash endowment to help pay the minister's salary for all time? It was given when they were in perfect health, and two of the donors still live. One of your members finished the chapel at Hanover and endowed a chair in memory of her mother, whose picture adorns this platform; another sitting before me gave them $1,000 in memory of Prof. Harrison Thomson, who hoed corn with him as a barefoot boy. Another gave Whitewater Presbytery $1,000 permanent home mission fund to help this corner of the State forever; and $1,000 to endow a chair at the table in Park College, on which some student can sit three times a day forever and gather nourishment for the body while seeking food for the mind. Now, without stopping to add together the many dollars we have expended at home in church and Sabbath-school work, and the sums gathered at special and in stated collections to help God's cause in other places, which would make a vast sum indeed, what has been done in these permanent ways is gratifying.

"The text bids me 'Walk about Zion, that ye may tell it to the generation following.' I am speaking to the generation following that noble band, and to many young families just starting in life who need but to look over this community to see that 'there is that scattereth and yet increaseth.' And look on other communities that have made no such provision for moral, intellectual and religious training to see that 'there is that that withholdeth more than is meet, and it tendeth to poverty.' Look upon this beautiful building, fresh from the frescoing and painting brush, that may stand for a century a monument to the liberal givers of Kingston, and as you go to your home, look upon the fine farms on every side, that speak of the industry and frugality of the pioneers, and say with David, 'The lines are fallen unto me in pleasant places; yea, I have a goodly heritage.'

"Taking in the whole range of thought in this discourse, and I have never seen a spot of earth that surpasses that which may be seen from the tower of this building, and there is no reason why you young people may not make the future Kingston Church surpass the one of the olden time. This house is the fourth evolution from the first log meeting-house, that stood over the way, and some are here to-day whose self-sacrifice helped build every one of the five, and these large brick dwellings were evolved from the little log cabins with puncheon floors and clapboard roofs. But the builders, with but a step between them and the grave, look across the valley of the shadow of death to the upper and better sanctuary where they will worship, and to the house not made with hands, eternal in the heavens; and bequeath to you this place of worship and your dwellings here, with desire that you make the next seventy-five years of church history surpass the last."

REV. DANIEL GILMER.

THE DIAMOND JUBILEE OF KINGSTON CHURCH.

" Let the people praise thee, O God ;
Let all the people praise thee."—Ps. 67:3.

REDEDICATORY SERVICE.

DOXOLOGY.
(Congregation standing.)

OPENING RESPONSE.

Pastor—Praise ye the Lord. Praise God in His sanctuary ; praise Him in the firmament of His power.

People—Praise Him for His mighty acts : praise Him according to His excellent greatness.

Pastor—Praise Him with the sound of the trumpet : praise Him with the psaltery and harp.

People—Praise Him with the timbrel and dance : praise Him with stringed instruments and organs.

Pastor—Praise Him upon the loud symbals : praise Him upon the high sounding cymbals.

People—Let everything that hath breath praise the Lord. Praise ye the Lord.

INVOCATION.
(Congregation seated.)

HYMN.

Great is the Lord our God,
  And let His praise be great ;
He makes His churches His abode,
  His most delightful seat.

These temples of His grace,
  How beautiful they stand !
The honors of our native place,
  The bulwarks of our land.

In Zion God is known,
  A refuge in distress ;
How bright has His salvation shone
  Through all her palaces !

Oft have our fathers told,
  Our eyes have often seen,
How well our God secures the fold
  Where His own sheep have been.

In every new distress
  We'll to His house repair,
We'll think upon His wondrous grace,
  And seek deliverance there.

(To be read in unison.)

Lift up your heads, O ye gates ;
And be ye lifted up, ye everlasting doors; and the King of Glory shall come in.

Who is this King of Glory? The Lord, strong and mighty, the Lord mighty in battle.

Lift up your heads, O ye gates ; even lift them up, ye everlasting doors; and the King of Glory shall come in.

Who is this King of Glory? The Lord of hosts, he is the King of Glory.

HYMN.
(Congregation standing.)

How beauteous on the mountains,
The feet of Him that brings
Like streams from living fountains,
Good tidings of good things ;
That publisheth salvation,
And jubilee release,
To every tribe and nation,
God's reign of joy and peace !

Lift up thy voice, O watchman !
And shout from Zion's towers,
Thy Hallelujah chorus,—
" The victory is ours !"
The Lord shall build up Zion
In glory and renown,
And Jesus, Judah's lion,
Shall wear His rightful crown.

Break forth in hymns of gladness,
O waste Jerusalem !
Let songs, instead of sadness,
Thy jubilee proclaim ;
The Lord, in strength victorious,
Upon thy foes hath trod ;
Behold ! O earth ! the glorious
Salvation of our God !

SCRIPTURE LESSON.

SPECIAL MUSIC.

REDEDICATORY PRAYER—PASTOR.

OFFERTORY.

REDEDICATORY SERMON—DR. A. T. RANKIN.

HYMN.
(Congregation standing.)

Zion ! awake, thy strength renew,
Put on thy robes of beauteous hue ;
And let the admiring world behold
The King's fair daughter clothed in gold.

Church of our God ! arise and shine,
Bright with the beams of truth divine :
Then shall thy radiance stream afar,
Wide as the heathen nations are.

Gentiles and kings thy light shall view,
And shall admire and love thee, too ;
They come like crowds across the sky,
As doves that to their window fly.

CLOSING RESPONSE.

Pastor—Grace be unto you, and peace, from Him which is, and which was, and which is to come ; and from the seven spirits which are before His throne.

People—And from Jesus Christ, who is the faithful witness, and the first begotten of the dead, and the Prince of the kings of the earth. Unto Him that loved us, and washed us from our sins in His own blood.

All—And hath made us kings and priests unto God, and His Father ; to Him be glory and dominion forever and ever, Amen.

BENEDICTION.

REV. A. T. RANKIN, D. D.

LIST OF ORIGINAL MEMBERS OF SAND CREEK CHURCH, AT KINGSTON.

ELDERS:

Samuel Donnell,
John Hopkins,

John C. McCoy,
Wm. O. Ross.

Paul Brown,	Nancy McCoy,	Hetty Jones,
Hannah Brown,	Sally Hopkins,	Elizabeth Henry,
Elijah Mitchel,	Charity Hamilton,	Jane Throp,
Fidelia Mitchel,	Aron Ardery,	Jane Hamilton,
Thomas Hamilton,	Samuel Donnell, Jr.,	Polly Hamilton,
Robert Donnell,	Caty Robison,	David Henry,
Clarisa Donnell,	Alexander McCoy,	Nancy Donnell, Jr.,
James Donnell,	Sarah Gageby,	Jane Hopkins,
Betsey Donnell,	Thomas Hendricks,	Caty Hopkins,
Josiah Collins,	Elizabeth Hendricks,	Elizabeth R. Ross,
Nelly Collins,	Margaret McCoy,	Julian Donnell,
Robert Thorne,	Nancy Antrobus,	John Antrobus,
Lydia Thorne,	Samuel D. Henry,	Isabella Antrobus,
Thomas Donnell,	Robert Hamilton,	Polly Antrobus,
Nancy Donnell,	Polly Hamilton,	Spica Thomson.
Polly Hamilton, Sr ,		

NOTE.

The following persons have filled the office of ruling elder in the Kingston church since the division in 1837, in addition to those given in the body of this paper as serving previous to that time. The dates of their election and retirement have been as carefully verified as is possible after this distance of time. Although the church for a year or more after the division was connected with the Congregational body, it immediately elected three elders—Samuel Donnell, John C. McCoy and Thomas Hamilton. The two former had served as elders in the old church since its organization in 1823, until dropped from the session on account of their anti-slavery sentiments in 1836. Thomas Hamilton, elected in 1829, had retired at the same time and for the same reason.

The list is as follows :

Samuel Donnell, elected 1837, resigned 1844 ; John C. McCoy, elected 1837, died 1865 ; Thomas Hamilton, elected 1837, died 1880 ; John C. Donnell, elected 1844, died 1883 ; Andrew Robison, Jr., elected 1844, died 1853 ; J. C. Adams, elected 1854, resigned 1869 ; Jesse G. Donnell, elected 1866 ; J. A. McCoy, elected 1866, removed from neighborhood 1889 ; G. D. Parker, elected 1866, removed from neighborhood 1867 ; J. B. Hopkins, elected 1869 ; S. H. Hamilton, elected 1881, removed from neighborhood 1885 ; Wm. H. Scott, elected 1881, died 1885 ; R. H. Evans, elected 1885, died 1891 ; J. B. Robison, elected 1886 ; Samuel Jackson, elected 1895 ; W. K. Stewart, elected 1895.

EXTRACTS FROM THOMAS HAMILTON'S HISTORY.

The following extracts from a history of the church prepared by Thomas Hamilton in 1857 present the personal recollections and opinions of one of the earliest and most devoted friends of the church. Uncle Tommy Hamilton, as he was familiarly called, possessed in a very remarkable degree the confidence and esteem of the entire neighborhood, both in and out of the church membership, during the fifty years of his service as elder. He died June 16, 1880. His manuscript was not available at the time of the anniversary, but some of its more interesting features are herewith subjoined :

" Having composed one of the number of those who were first organized into the Sand Creek church, and having been familiar with and having taken a deep interest in everything connected with her welfare for a third of a century, it seemed good to me to give an outline of the most important events connected with its history for the benefit of those who may come after, that they may shun the mistakes and improve whatever may be worthy of imitation. The church was organized in the latter part of 1823, by Rev. John R. Moreland. The name at first given was Concord, afterward changed to the present name on account of some other church in the State having the same name.

" The original membership was mainly emigrants from Kentucky and Pennsylvania, mostly from Concord Church in the former State. Some from the first organization of that State had labored for the abolition of slavery. Despairing of success, and unwilling that their descendents should grow up under the blighting influence of the iniquitous system, they concluded, though even then advanced in life, to leave that rich, fertile and healthy land for one less so, that they and theirs might enjoy the advantages of free institutions. The country was passing through the most unprecedented pressure experienced since the Revolutionary struggle. Prices, during a few years preceding, had ruled high. A great amount of bank paper had been put in circulation without any capital, and a general breaking-down ensued. Almost the whole country was in debt. Well-improved land in Kentucky came down from twenty-five dollars to eight dollars an acre, and other property in proportion. Most of the early settlers had but little capital over what purchased their land, and owned but small tracts. The country was covered at that time with a dense growth of green beech, sugar and other trees of enormous size, few farms having more than ten acres partly cleared. The seasons at that time were very wet, especially in the winter and spring. There being no underdraining, the best part of our lands were lost. Several years passed before enough was raised for home consumption. At that time there was no school or meeting-house, but meetings for prayer and conference were held regularly, conducted for the most part by Samuel Donnell and John Hopkins.

" In the summer of 1825 a site for a church and burying ground was selected. The congregation met and felled the trees and burned the brush and part of the logs on about an acre of ground, then took a subscription from individuals for a house, each one agreeing to furnish a certain number of logs, rafters, sleepers, shingles, etc., and some small sums of money to pay for lumber, nails and carpenter work. Nothing was done to the church that season but to raise to the square. In the fall of 1825 Rev. S. G. Lowry visited the church with a view of settlement. With some aid from the A. H. M. S., an amount was raised sufficient for his support, and some aid to purchase for him eighty acres of land. He accordingly settled in December, 1825. During the winter the congregation met, hewed logs and raised a house on his own land about half a mile from the church."

Mr. Hamilton describes the ministry of Mr. Lowry as successful, and attended with two or three revivals and a camp-meeting conducted by Rev. Alexander Rankin. During this period they organized under the common school system ; and the first temperance movement was begun under the auspices of Mr. Lowry and a Mr. Strange. He speaks of Mr. Lowry as a moderate New School man, and his resignation, in 1832, as brought about partly by ill health and partly by the opposition of the Old School element in the church. His successor, Rev. J. S. Weaver, was a pronounced Old School minister. The narrative continues :

"The pressure of the times had gradually given way. Farms were made ; farmers had some surplus, and rude cabins were giving way to more comfortable and permanent houses. While this was the case on the farms, it was thought the rude, uncomfortable log church should be replaced by a better. Accordingly, funds were raised by subscription and the building of a brick house let to the lowest bidder. During the building of the church, the anti-slavery movement began to be agitated here. A country society, auxiliary to the American Anti-slavery Society, was organized. Few of the members of the church manifested any hostility to the abolition movement. All joined in condemning slavery ; but a considerable part stood aloof or refused active co-operation. Abolitionists became zealous, as opposition increased, pressed their arguments by means of lectures, newspapers and tracts, until to a great extent that became the absorbing topic of interest. The pastor, seeing that a portion, perhaps a majority of the church were not abolitionists, began to stand aloof, or rather attempted to occupy neutral ground. In the meantime, the abolitionists, being so indubitably convinced of the truth and importance of their principles, became impatient to some extent, thought all good and right-minded men ought to embrace them, and occasionally were led into some imprudences. About this time, Mr. Hopkins was candidate for the State Legislature again. Most, if not all, the anti-slavery members refused to support him on account of his want of co-operation in the temperance and anti-slavery movements, which somewhat chagrined him, he having always heretofore received their support."

Mr. Hamilton here gives an account of the differences between Mr. Hopkins and the session, growing out of this candidacy, which are given fully in the old session book, and proceeds :

" Up to this time no very active opposition had obtained in the church to the anti-slavery movement, but from this time, efforts were made to create parties for and against the movement. The state of the public mind was such that all who embraced the temperance and anti-slavery causes did it at the cost of all hope of preferment to office. Many, from a general desire to stand well with others, thinking their influence in society would be impaired, and that the abolitionists went too far and too fast, hereafter stood aloof from the cause."

Mr. Hamilton's account of the events leading up to the division, and of the subsequent history of the church, is too long to be conveniently quoted here. Perhaps enough has been given to show the tolerant and just spirit in which our most notable church controversy is reviewed by one of the most earnest participants in it

REV. J. A. LIGGITT, D. D.

HISTORY OF REV. JOHN R. MORELAND, WHO ORGANIZED THE OLD SAND CREEK CHURCH.

By Dr. W. B. Wishard, of Indianapolis.

"Rev. John R. Moreland was born in 1785 in western Pennsylvania. He grew up with no educational advantages except those afforded by the school taught in a log house. He was a carpenter, and as there was little to do in that time, he took to flat-boating to New Orleans. When twenty-one or twenty-two years old, he walked home through the Indian nations, a journey of about nine hundred miles.

" On one of his trips down the Ohio river, he stopped three or four days at Limestone, now Maysville, Ky. The Rev. Dr. Lyle, an eminent divine of Kentucky, was holding a protracted meeting in the Presbyterian church. He went to hear him, and was so much interested that when they were ready to start the boat, he notified his crew he would not run the boat any more. He stated to the crew that he was converted, and that his life plan was changed. The revival was one of unusual power, and he caught the fire that was never lost during his noble ministry. After the meeting was closed, he visited in Mercer County, Ky. His means were limited. He attended Transylvania College, Lexington, Ky. It is my impression that he never graduated. When he returned, he commenced studying divinity with the celebrated Thomas Clelland, D. D., of Mercer county. The Rev. Thornton A. Mills, D. D., and the Rev. James A. Carnahan, while visiting at my home, spoke enthusiastically of Mr. Moreland. In 1848 I had occasion to visit Kentucky, and saw many of his old acquaintances. One of them, who had often heard him, stated that he could command larger congregations than anyone who had ever preached in that county. He was a man of great muscular strength and endurance ; he was an uncompromising enemy of slavery ; this was his reason for leaving Kentucky.

"There were several of his old acquaintances living in Indianapolis. They invited him to visit them. The First church was vacant. He received a call and came here in December, 1828. On week days he preached wherever opportunity presented itself. He preached extemporaneously from notes. But a few days since one of our retired attorneys, a former judge of the court, spoke to me of his preaching. He said his appeals to the unconverted were the strongest he had ever heard, and at such time he shed tears, and melted the congregation.

" He died suddenly, in October, 1832, and now sleeps in Green Lawn Cemetery. The church erected a stone — there were no monuments in that day.

SERMON BY HARRY NYCE,

*At the Seventy-fifth Anniversary of the Presbyterian Church,
at Kingston, Indiana.*

"When the Rev. Mr. Bartlett informed me, at the meeting of synod, of the coming celebration of the seventy-fifth anniversary of the Kingston church, I at once said: 'I would like to be present.' I well recall the being present at the semi-centennial anniversary. I hope that twenty-five years hence, at the centennial anniversary, many of the boys and girls here to-day will recall as vividly this seventy-fifth anniversary as some recall that which occurred twenty-five years ago.

"Your minister asked me to speak to you to-day. Since the history of the church has been so well recalled, by those who have contributed to the making of that history, at this closing hour of the day I desire to speak to you from the text found in the second chapter and in the tenth verse of the Gospel, according to the apostle John: 'Thou hast kept the good wine until now.'

"These words are taken from the account given by the Apostle John of the first miracle of Jesus in Cana of Gallilee. A wedding had taken place, and the guests were happy and contented at the supper, for, by the power of the miracle-working guest, the water had been turned into wine. The ruler of the feast came and tasted the water that was made wine. He knew not whence it was. He thought that the bridegroom was responsible for the wine. He tells how the good wine had been kept until toward the end of the feast. Usually it comes at the beginning. The ruler of the feast says to the bridegroom: 'Every man at the beginning doth set forth good wine, and when men have well drunk then that which is worse; but thou hast kept the good wine until now.' 'Thou hast kept the good wine until now.' The words of the ruler only referred to the feast in Cana of Gallilee. But the words are also true of the religion of Jesus Christ, who worked His first miracle at that marriage feast. The words of the ruler, 'thou hast kept the good wine until now,' were wiser than he who uttered them knew. Stand-ing as we do to-day, in the last month of the year, let us have these words teach us lessons of the religion of Christ. May we not ask at this anniver-sary time if it is true in the world at large, and if it is true in our own lives, that the best is coming last? We are now drawing very near to the close of the nineteenth century. Soon 1900 years since the birth of Christ will have been completed. The religion of Christ has had time to accomplish some-thing in the world at large and in the hearts of men. If the ruler of the feast were alive to-day and would recall not merely the power of Jesus at that wedding so long ago in Cana of Gallilee, but if he could look out upon a world in which the power of Christianity has been working for 1900 years; if he could look into the experiences of your life and my life to the time of this seventy-fifth anniversary of the Kingston church, would he say: 'Thou hast kept the good wine until now?' Let us ask then to-day: Is the world growing better or worse? Am I, as an individual, becoming better, stronger in Christ as the years come and go? Do we look back to-day upon the world at the time when Christ was born and say that the world was better then than it is now? Roman and Grecian mythology saw their golden age in the past. The religion of the Jews and that of the Christians found their golden age in the future, not in the past. Adam and Eve were driven out of paradise, but the prophets and the psalmists did not look back upon the lost joys of paradise; they ever looked 'forward to the transcendent glories of the kingdom of the Messiah.' We wonder and are put to shame by the devotion and courage of the disciples to the cause of Christ, for we some-times wonder if we, as Christians, to-day could endure imprisonment and martyrdom as they endured. The earnestness and the devotedness of the few—of Paul and of John, of Matthew and Mark—may have been greater than the earnestness of Christians to-day; but, nevertheless, the sin of man was great in that day. The letters of the apostles tell of widespread sin and guilt on the part of man, and they looked forward into the future when Christ would have come again; when the power of Christ would have worked in the world; when the Gentiles would have turned unto the Cross of Christ. Yes; in the Old and in the New Testament, the golden age was to be in the future and not in the past. The best wine of the feast was to be kept until the last.

"And as the world grows older, better things are given to man. Surely in a material sense this is so. Viewing the comforts of life, the triumphs of art and invention, no man in his senses would rather have lived in 1798 than in 1898. No man would want to place himself back in 1823, or 1698, or in the Year of Our Lord 98, to live merely regarding the material comforts of men. Mother Shipton, who is said to have lived in England in the sixteenth century, uttered her prophecy concerning material things. Living three hundred and fifty years after her famous prophecy was uttered, let us notice how much of that prophecy has been fulfilled in a material way :

> "Carriages without horses shall go,
> And accidents fill the world with woe.
> Around the world thoughts shall fly
> In the twinkling of an eye.
> Waters shall yet more wonders do;
> Now strange, yet shall be true.
> Through hills man shall ride
> And no horse or ass be at his side.
> Under water, man shall walk,
> Shall ride, shall read, shall talk;
> Iron sha'l in the water float
> As easy as a boat
> Gold shall be found, and known and shown,
> In a land that is not known.
> Fire and water shall wonders do;
> England at last admit a Jew.
> The world to an end shall come
> In eighteen hundred and eighty-one."

> "The world to an end shall come
> In eighteen hundred and eighty-one "

"This did not occur, but much of the rest of the strange prophecy has occurred. The power of steam, the telegraph, the telephone, the electric light, the electric motor and many other inventions have made the comforts of living greater at the end of this century than at any other time in the world's history. It is glorious to live at a time when thought can be transmitted around the earth. In the Midwinter Night's Dream, Shakespeare causes his fancy to play, and Puck says: 'I'll put a girdle about the earth in forty minutes.' The fancy of the poet has almost become a fact in science, for, in May, 1896, at the electrical exposition in New York, this message was started around the world: 'God creates, nature treasures, science utilizes electrical power for the grandeur of nations and the peace of the world.' These words were started at 8:35; at 9:25, just fifty minutes from the start, the receiving instrument clicked, and the message was taken exactly as sent, having made a trip of 27,500 miles. Surely it is more convenient to live in such a time than in the time when battles were fought since the opposing armies had received no intelligence that a treaty of peace was concluded.

"Great has been the advance in science, art and invention during the century drawing to a close. But we would not dwell upon the material advancement to-day. As one says, 'it is surely more convenient to strike a light with a friction match than with a tinder box.' But the burglar who uses the friction match in the nineteenth century is just as much a criminal as the bandit of the twelfth century who used the tinder box. Starting as we did to-day with the text, 'Thou hast kept the good wine until now,' we would ask the question, Is the moral life of the world better as the years go on? Is the world growing better? Is it true that the good wine of the world is being kept until now?

" Let us look first at the trust of man in his fellow man. We look to-day at the business arrangements of the world, and we find that they depend in a large measure upon honor. Edward Everett Hale tells us that in the first century in the days of Augustus Cæsar, and even in the twelfth century, in the days of Richard Cœur de Lion, the trade of the world was not conducted as it is to-day. In those days when a man sold his goods he went with his goods to protect them and to see that he got a return for his goods when delivered. The tradesman was a peddler. Think to-day of the vast volume of exchange in the world which rests upon honor. A tradesman lets his goods go out of his sight and trusts often simply upon a promise to pay. He sends his goods to a distant part of the country, or across wide, wide seas, and expects with certainty to receive a return from men he has never seen. Is not this trust of man in his fellow man so widespread and so essential a part of the commerce of to-day a sign that the world is better than it was? Does not an extended system of business credit exist to-day since man has been taught by the religion of Christ to trust his fellow man ?

" Again, a sign that the world is becoming better at the close of this century is the interest of man in his fellow man. Workers, though they may belong to the poorer classes, are not regarded as so many hands, but as souls, as brother men. A writer, in the New York Independent, who was asked last summer to give the most striking characteristic of Queen Victoria's sixty years reign, gave the answer most aptly by a quotation taken from a story by Lord Beaconsfield, the story of Sybil, placed in the year of the Queen's accession.

" 'This is a new reign,' said Egremont ; 'perhaps it is a new era.'

" 'I think so,' said the younger stranger.

" 'I hope so,' said the older one.

" 'Well, society may be in its infancy,' said Egremont, slightly smiling, 'but say what you like, our Queen reigns over the greatest nation that ever existed.'

" 'Which nation ?' asked the younger stranger, 'for she reigns over two.'

" The stranger paused; Egremont was silent, but looked inquiringly.

" 'Yes, resumed the younger stranger, after a moment's interval, two nations; between whom there is no intercourse and no sympathy; who are as ignorant of each other's habits, thoughts and feelings as if they were dwellers in different zones, or inhabitants of different planets, who are formed by a different breeding, are fed by a different food, are ordered by different manners, and are not governed by the same laws.'

" 'You speak of,' said Egremont, hesitatingly.

" 'The rich and the poor.'

" A sure sign that the world is becoming better to-day is the interest of these two nations, the interest of the rich and the poor, the one in the other. Years ago nobody outside of a few distressed himself about the condition of the poor. Now it is a healthy sign that men do distress themselves; 'that children are being freed from degrading toil; that sympathy with the suffering and poor is more deep and full.' The world has still many problems to solve, but that the world has begun in earnest to work upon the solution of its problems is a most healthful sign of the progress of the times. The year 1898 has granted unto history the spectacle of a great nation going forth in behalf of others, ready to make the sacrifice of war, not for itself, but for others.

" In seeking the solution of these problems there is a larger fraternal spirit among men than ever before. We are told: 'That once upon a large ocean steamer, with seven hundred passengers from different classes of society, there came a sudden calamity. The main shaft of the engine broke; great holes were made in the bottom of the vessel, and three compartments were filled with water. There was extreme danger that all on board would perish. All classes mingled freely. Of course there was fear; but during all the time of great trial the people were kind to one another. Prejudices of race and condition did not appear to hinder that spirit of the Great Master, which teaches men to be helpful one to the other.' I believe that scene is characteristic of the race at large. Great trials will come to men, but in the midst of it all people will seek to be helpful to the other. The development of the altruistic feeling on the part of humanity tells us that the world is growing better and not worse.

" Many are the ways in which we might ask you to verify the truth, that since the birth of Jesus Christ in Bethlehem, the world is growing better.

" Of course, if we look for it, we can find much that is evil, much of sin and crime in the world; but also there is much that is good and pure. An English critic, Mr. Stead, has written strongly of the sin in New York and Chicago; nevertheless I doubt not but that much concerning the higher and better life of these two cities could be written, of the influence of the churches in these cities, teaching a moral code wholesome alike for body and soul; telling man of his relation to his fellow man. We might also look at the care of the sick in the hospitals of these cities, of the care of the blind, the deaf, the dumb, the lame and the insane. We might glance at the higher life of these cities as manifested in the libraries and galleries; we might, in passing, notice the public school system, where an education is placed within the reach of all the children. Yes, there is much that is good to be found by him who will only seek for the good.

" If we have our minds open we can behold the progress of the world on all sides. As you go into Greensburg, your county seat, you behold the tower of your court-house. Think how the justice administered in that court-house has been transformed by the influence of the Babe of Bethlehem. The justice administered there has a theory of family life that did not come from Roman jurisprudence, but from the commandments of Moses and from the treasure of Christian truth found in the Holy Scriptures. No plea at all could be heard in that court-house of the absolute ownership of the man over the woman that can be heard to-day in a Mohammedan or Turkish civilization. Never for a moment in that court-house can be advanced to-day pleas for the justification of human slavery. Who would maintain in that court-house the principle of the absolute rights of a ruler, that a ruler or king had absolute ownership over his subjects and their belongings? Many are the principles of justice administered to-day in your court-house, the inspiration of which is found in the religion of Christ.

"Great is the sinfulness of to-day, but there were sins in the time of the Apostle Paul, for which we have no names to-day. Read the first chapter of Romans and you will know the condition of the world in the time of the Apostle Paul. And we believe that since certain sins are unknown the condition of the world is better to-day. It is said that 'on the shore of Lake Erie you can see that the land relatively to the water is rising, or that the water is receding as time rolls on. Three or four parallel ridges of sand mark the successive boundaries of the lake, and now towns and villages and railways appear, and thousands of acres of farm lands where once only a waste of water appeared.' So it is with the moral conditions of mankind. Where once there was a waste of human slavery there now arise the dignity and worth of true manhood; where once there were sins, names for which we do not have; interest for man, the care and culture of men, these things have supplanted evil things, and the world is growing better, not worse. As we stand at this anniversary time in the last month of the year 1898 and view the progress of mankind, are not the words of the pastor of the Pilgrim Fathers being fulfilled, for as they sailed from Delft in 1620 he said: 'I am convinced that the Lord hath yet more truth for us, yet to break forth out of His Holy Word.' That truth is breaking forth upon us, and God will ever have a higher, better, nobler life for those of his children who choose to place themselves in line with that which He is ever revealing to the children of men. The question for you and me to ask at this anniversary time is: 'Am I in line with God's purposes for his children, am I being exalted and blessed by his purposes, or are the years coming and going, yesterday 1897, to-day 1898, to-morrow 1899, without my life being a blessing to God and to mankind? Am I setting myself against Jesus Christ, the Revealer of God's will? Have I confessed Him before men?' As we have tried to answer the question that God is causing His world to become better, may each of us try to answer to-day a more practical question, which is, Am I becoming better? As I grow older is the best wine being kept for me at the feast's end?

" It is true that God intends life to become better, richer and deeper as life grows old. The literature of to-day calls childhood 'The Golden Age,' but Kenneth Grahame, Barrie and Stevenson, we think, are mistaken. Childhood is not the richest, the best time of life. The best time of life for the Christian should be the time when life is rich with past experiences. The golden wedding is placed after fifty years of married life in Christian lands, the diamond in still later years; not because the husband and wife have many more years in which to enjoy either gold or diamonds, but because gold and diamonds symbolize best the richness of their love together during many years, and that the golden time is at the end and not at the beginning of their days. Is it not true with the religion of Christ that the best comes as life becomes older? The man of the world says, 'Let me get all out of life now. Soon degenerate days will come. I am sure only of this present day. Let me get all I can out of it. Old age must be very dreary, and desolate. Therefore, I will dissipate now and get all I can without regard to old age or to a life beyond the grave.' This may be the view of the man of the world, of that one who is not a Christian. But said Phillips Brooks, in a sermon upon the text of to-day, to which I am indebted, 'The essence of Christianity is to believe that the world is growing better; that the life of man is growing better under the discipline of Christ. It is calm and hopeful with its great assurances. It sets the old man, at the end of his career, in the midst of fulfilled promises and finished educations, splendidly saying, as he looks back over his life, "It has all been good, but this is the best of all. Thou, O Christ, O Master, hast kept the good wine until now."'

" As with the world at large, so God intends it to be with each human life. Looking back to-day at the close of the nineteenth century, we can not think of any century that has been better than this century. With your knowledge of history, will you say to-day that you would rather have lived in any previous century than this, since that was a better century? So, also, God intends life to become better, richer to us as the years are better. As a Christian man or woman looking back over your years you ought not to be able to say that any previous year was better than this year. In the allotted course of human life, three score and ten, God grants unto soul and body many years in this world. Is it not a wonderful thing that a human body, with its delicate organization, should go on sleeping and working, toiling and breathing, without intermission and without rest, for seventy, eighty, ninety years? Could any machine ever constructed by man sustain such a constant, uninterrupted action for that length of time? If God permits the machine to run so long is there not a purpose in the running? If the faith of man is ever strong in him, he grants richer, deeper experiences to the soul as each year comes and goes. I believe it is so. Did not life mean more to Gladstone in his old age than it did in the year 1819 to Gladstone, the boy, at ten years of age? Our Savior did not live to be an old man, but we read, as the years came and passed away, that he 'increased in wisdom and stature, and in favor with God and man.' Life was richer and deeper to Jesus Christ at Nazareth, on the sea of Galilee, at Gethsemane, in Jerusalem, and on Calvary than it was to Him as a babe in Bethlehem. As God gave to His own Son, so to all his children in Jesus Christ He will ever give a richer, deeper knowledge of Himself as the years come and go. As a father, if I have a valuable watch I cannot give it to my little boy until my boy understands the value of the watch and knows how to take care of it. Your Father in heaven cannot give His blessings to His child until that child is ready by discipline, by faith, by trust made stronger, and by experience made deeper, to receive His blessings. At this season of the giving of gifts, you might rush out into the street and thrust a ten-dollar bill into a man's hands, saying, ' Here, this is yours.' You could then leave him in full possession of the bill. But you cannot rush up to that man and thrust a character upon him. To gain a character, to gain a sure and constant faith, to know the promises of God as tried and not found wanting, the years must come and go. And tell me, you of middle age and you of old age, you who have had faith in your Master, lo these many years, is not the best wine, that is, the strongest hope, the most abiding faith at the feast's end? Blessed it is to see an aged Christian saying, after all the trials and sorrows of life, ' Yes, though He slay me, yet will I trust Him.' Contrast with this, the life of one who has dissipated in youth and lived a life of sin, and then lived fifty, sixty, seventy years without faith and without prayer, without God in the world. And then he passes into eternity without hope. The life of sin has no happy old men ; and the word of God tells that they are not happy in the world beyond. But in the world beyond, for him who lives with faith in Christ there is joy. There, there, the good wine is kept. The true completion of this life is in the life to come. 'I will come again and receive you to myself.' 'I will dwell in the house of the Lord forever.' 'And so shall we be ever with the Lord.' ' Now we see through a glass darkly, but then face to face.' 'It doth not yet appear what we shall be, but we know that when He shall appear we shall be like Him.' 'Let not your heart be troubled. Ye believe in God. Believe also in me. In my Father's house are many mansions. If it were not so I would have told you. I go to prepare a place for you, and if I go and prepare a place for you, I will come again and receive you unto myself ; that where I am, there ye may be also.' All these words look forward. They tell of that which Jesus has in store for us. Let us realize that many are the blessings there, as many and great have been the blessings here. We are all nearing that home beyond. Some have passed into His eternal glory this year. For some, the voyage of life in this world may close next year. Some of our aged fathers and mothers feel that it is not long now with them. Weakened physical health, faltering step, diminished physical vigor, tell that the time of departure is near at hand. But the hope of the soul is strong ; God has been precious to them in the past, and they believe that He has still more glory to reveal unto them. Even now they are looking forward with anticipation to the life beyond.

" When death was before Charles Kingsley, he said, 'God forgive me, but I look forward to it with intense and reverent curiosity.' Did not his curiosity fulfill his human nature, knowing that as God had dealt with him in the past so would He deal with him in the future, and still greater glory would be manifested unto him? After a long ocean voyage, a'ter the ship has been out many days, when she is coming near the port and the harbor, the passengers are all interested in the new land; in that which the new and hitherto unknown land will have in store for them. They speak of their preparation for landing, of their interest of the new life which will be on the shore. On this anniversary day we are all nearing port; we are all one year nearer. Some are twenty, thirty, forty, fifty, sixty, seventy, eighty years nearer than ever before. Perhaps even next year the glory of that port to which we are journeying will be revealed to us. May we so live during the voyage that much of His love can be revealed now, and we may rest assured that new and greater things shall be in store for us there. There we shall be with Jesus Christ ; there we shall see loved ones who have gone before. There, there shall be no more pain, no more sin. There we shall forever be with the Lord in the city of our God. There, we believe that the words of the ruler of the feast unto the bridegroom will be fully realized by each child of God. ' Thou hast kept the good wine until now.' "

EXTRACTS FROM LETTERS.

*Letter from Mrs. Carpenter and Mrs. Mannon, daughters of
Rev. Daniel Gilmer.*

We feel that we are paying a tribute of affection and respect to our
father's memory in recalling the membership and work of the Kingston
church during the years of his pastorate. It also gives us pleasure to call to
mind the friends of our youth, though many of them, especially the older
members of the church, are resting from their earthly labors. We remember
them as they filled their places in the old frame church, forty years ago.
Of your pastor at that time, we will only say, in the words of a member of
your church, "I remember him as an honest, fearless defender of the truth,
and always foremost in the ranks."

One who was always prominent in good works was Uncle Tommy Hamilton, an elder at that time, for whom father had a warm affection. He spoke
of him as one of the most conscientious men he ever knew. Uncle John
McCoy was another, always in his place at the Sunday services and prayer-
meeting, while on week days he made visits among the different homes,
where he was always welcome on account of his genial good nature and
pleasant manner. Uncle Alex McCoy led the music the first two or three
years we were at Kingston. Doubtless many will remember how he led off on
the good old tunes, Coronation, Ortonville, Balerma, and many others. Later
on, we had a singing school taught by Mr. Harvey, and shortly after, John
Robison became the leader of the church music. Soon after he took charge
of the music, the synod of the Free Presbyterian church met at Kingston.
As this was an important occasion, the young people formed a choir and sang
set pieces and anthems, as well as the regular psalms and hymns. As there
were a great many young people in the church, the social element was an
important factor. We remember no other place where there were so many
natural advantages for innocent amusements. The blue-grass pastures,
shaded by forest trees, furnished ideal places for picnics in summer ; and as
with well-filled baskets we drove through the shady lanes to some common
meeting-place for the young people of the neighborhood, we enjoyed life in
full measure. On winter nights we went sleighing and gathered in some one
of the numerous homes, where we always met a hearty welcome, and beside
the wide fireplace, and often overflowing from the living-room into other
rooms, we enjoyed ourselves in many ways known to young people of that
day. During the winter of 1856-57, there was serious apprehension on the
part of pastor and elders that some of the younger members were indulging
in amusements not consistent with church membership. There was some
talk of discipline, but Uncle Tommy Hamilton plead for a special effort to
bring the young people back to their first love. During the preceding summer, a course of lectures from the Hebrews had been given by the pastor,
which were no doubt scholarly and edifying to the older members, but at
this time a different direction was given the preaching of the word, and
God's love and mercy were feelingly presented. These sermons, supple-
mented by the prayers of such men as Uncle Tommy Hamilton and others,
brought about the desired result and the wandering ones returned to the

fold. Thus forty years ago in the old frame church at Kingston was preached the same truth, now preached from many pulpits in our land as the new theology, having for its foundation, "God is love."

So from the Pacific coast, we send words of greeting, with kind remembrances of the past and words of hope and good cheer for the future. That you may live up to the high standard set by your forefathers, and like them, when your work is ended, enter into the joys of eternal life, is the sincere wish of your old-time friends.

HELENA GILMER MANNON, Pasadena, Cal.
MARY GILMER CARPENTER, Los Angeles, Cal.

TOPEKA, KANSAS, November 12, 1898.

My Dear Friends: I send you greetings on this interesting anniversary. Would that I might be with you and give them in person.

Our fathers builded well. All honor to their memory. My earliest recollection is of the church built of logs. Now you have the beautiful, modern church, with its spire pointing heavenward. Then we went to Sunday-school in the morning, followed by two long services with an intermission between. Later, at home in the evening the catechism was recited. Now, in this fast age, this would be called barbarous. But I do not remember of dreading the day, with all its lengthy services.

I have many tender memories connected with the Kingston church. There, in my girlhood, I found my Saviour, who is more and more precious as the years go by. There, later on, I gave my children to God in baptism, and in their maturer years they all came into full membership in the church. Some of them are privileged to tell "the old, old story of Jesus and His love" to those who have never heard. There, too, resting in the silent city near by, lies the earthly tabernacle of beloved husband, father, mother and kindred dear, awaiting the resurrection. Also many memories come of the loved, faithful pastor of so many years, going in and out among us in all our joys and in all our sorrows. What could be more fitting than that he should be with you on this occasion? No one could fill the place so well. May the blessing of the Lord abide on him and his, wherever their lot is cast. Also in the dear old church, may his banner ever her belove.

Always yours very sincerely,
MRS. N. H. ADAMS.

KINGMAN, KANSAS, December 13, 1898.

My first distinct recollection of the church is, when I was quite a child, we worshiped in the little frame church and Rev. Benj. Nyce was pastor. I do not remember much about the services, except the Sunday-school. I, with my sister and cousins, in company with Grandfather Donnell, walked to Sunday-school in nice weather, and rode home with the family after church. That was the custom in those days. Sunday-school was always at 9:00 o'clock, and I think there were never any tardy ones.

My teacher was Miss Margaret Hamilton, afterward Mrs. McCoy. To me she was the most beautiful and best woman in the world. Later, it was her sister Nancy who became Mrs. Adams ; and sometimes Melissa Hamilton, afterward Mrs. Nyce, was my teacher. Mr. Nyce made the Sunday-school

REV. HARRY NYCE.

very attractive by his talks to children. They were principally stories from
the Bible, told in a very charming way. I was so interested and impressed
that I became a Bible student. As I grew older, I found much in the Bible
to interest me besides stories. I remember in particular hearing him tell the
story of Elijah meeting the prophets of Baal, and calling down fire from
heaven to consume the sacrifice. I. Kings, 18th chapter.

Mr. Nyce had the faculty of making friends with the children, and I
always greeted with delight his visits to our home. He would take me on
his knee and tell me some beautiful story, and then laugh so gleefully that
it dispelled my shyness and established a confidence, and he was ever afterward my ideal of a Christian gentleman. I am sure a friendship began then
that in later years, as we stood in the relation of teacher and pupil, became
real, and which lasted as long as he lived, as his occasional letters and
papers, with especially marked columns, sent to me in my Western home
years afterward testified. He was eminently a friend of young people, and
during his second pastorate in the church he kept up a Bible class for the
young people at 4:00 o'clock Sunday afternoon during the winter months,
and made it so interesting that it was always well attended.

I also remember, as they came in succession, Rev. Adams, Joseph Monfort, Mr. King and Mr. Stryker. To my mind, they were very different and
had their own peculiar styles of preaching. I shall never forget Mr Monfort's beautiful singing. He sang the hymn beginning "Servant of God,
well done ; rest from thy loved employ," at Grandfather Donnell's funeral,
and as he sat in the pulpit and sang the entire hymn alone, I thought it
beautiful.

Among the ministers' wives I had some warm friends, one of whom was
Mrs. Stryker. Many a time have I, as a school-girl, stayed over night with
her for company when Mr. Stryker was gone to synod or Presbytery. She
was a lady of culture, and exerted a good influence over me. I remember
Mr. Cable more particularly in regard to the respect and friendship he always
extended to Grandfather Donnell than from anything else. He often visited
Grandfather, and I was quite frequently an interested listener, as they talked
on religious and church matters. In my estimation, he was a learned man.

Among the pleasant recollections of those days, I recall the annual visits
of Rev. Henry Little, of Madison, at which times we often had a series of
meetings, and I shall always remember his kind, earnest appeals to sinners,
and especially to young people.

Our prayer-meetings in those early days were quite a feature of the
church. It it true, I believe, that there never was much of a crowd there,
but there were a few who were always present, rain or shine, summer and
winter. Among the faithful were Uncle Tommy Hamilton, Uncle J. C. Mc-
Coy, Uncle Andy Robison and Uncle Addison Donnell. The young people
had a habit of attending quite regularly, and were respectful listeners,
although they took no active part except in the singing. Uncle Tommy
Hamilton and J. C. McCoy always prayed, and others as they were called
upon. The services, which never lasted over an hour, were as genuinely enjoyed by those present as if the house had been well filled, and in fact I think
Uncle Tommy Hamilton was serenely unconscious of the empty seats, and I
used to think he would have gone ahead with the meeting if there had been
no one present to take part but himself.

In the year 1848, during the pastorate of Rev. B. Franklin, Rev. Father Dickey conducted a revival meeting, and on the 26th day of February of that year, I and twelve other young people united with the church. I do not now remember who they were except my sister, Martha Donnell, Kate McCoy and Samuel H. Hamilton. I was younger than any of them, and was strongly advised by a friend not to do so foolish a thing as to join the church. I might try to be good and after while become a Christian, but it was not the proper thing to take children into the church. I did not take that view of the case, and was received with the others.

I cannot close this paper without paying a loving tribute to one of my Sunday-school teachers, Mrs. Eliza Jane Thomson, who taught a class of girls, of which I was one, for several years in the old brick church. During that time I do not remember of her being absent even once, and she was always on time. How faithful and patient she was! And I have sometimes thought how dull she must have thought us, for we allowed her to do all the talking. We would commit verses and recite whole chapters from memory, and do anything she required, but we did not seem to answer questions very well ; but we remembered much of what she taught, and it strongly influenced for good our after lives. ZERELDA DONNELL LAWSON.

———

LOCKPORT, N. Y., December 8, 1898.

To the Pastor and Members of the Dear Church at Kingston : It is a joy to me to send a letter to you to-day, a regret that I cannot intrude my presence. I know that the occasion will be like one of Sam Weller's muffins, "very fillin' for the price." My brother, Harry, is doubtless with you ; he is big enough for two, and I know, more full of feelings than fluent speech. Two of the Nyces have had the honor of serving the dear church, and my time may yet come when you can't get anybody else.

I owe more to the Kingston church than to any other. It was there I learned my first religious teaching, and found the way to our blessed Christ ; it is there, too, I hope to be taken and laid to rest with the dear ones across the way when my work is done. Some of my dearest childhood memories are connected with the old church. I can see the Rankins cross the road, file in one by one, usually more than less. A kindly word from the honored and faithful Rev. A. T. Rankin, or a gentle admonition from him, that Sunday is not the day to sit on the fence and whistle. "Boys, it is time for the service to begin." I remember well the organ and choir in the middle of the church ; the impression made upon my child ear by John Robison's voice still remains. James and Marshall and Cyrus Hamilton were to me patriarchs in those days. In building the new church, I thought that Lowry Donnell was the master builder and architect of the world. I have since seen St. Peter's at Rome, and the Milan and Cologne's Cathedrals. Yet they were not so beautiful as was to the child mind the dear church at home.

What a noble record it has had ; what influences have gone from it ; how the best and tenderest experiences of our lives have been received there ! May she, under her faithful pastor and your consecrated co-operation, continue to be the sanctifior of the community, the comfort of the sorrowing, the light to the darkened, the hope to the penitent, ever the dwelling of the living God. Yours in the noblest service,

BENJ. M. NYCE.

REV. R. A. BARTLETT.

SPRINGDALE, ARK., December 14, 1898.

Dear Brother Bartlett: Your letter of November 18th, inviting me to attend the seventy-fifth anniversary of the Kingston Church, was duly received. It found me in very poor health, added to the natural infirmity ordinarily weighing on a man of eighty-one years. But as you had kindly given me plenty of time, I hoped for better health and intended to respond, recalling incidents, events and persons, the kind of material with which it was organized, trained mostly by that orthodox, consecrated minister, Rev. John Rankin. I should tell how it prospered, largely by emigration, under that good Brother Lowry, and how subsequently, and as I think, for want of true Christian forbearance about non-essentials, animosities were aroused, feelings alienated, heated controversies.

The language was not such as Job 6:25 describes. How forcible are right words! They forgot "A soft answer turneth away wrath." The fruit of all this was division. And then two churches, composed largely of good, Christian people, orthodox, pious and more than average mental ability.

My work began in 1844 and continued eight years, the longest pastorate, I think, up to that date, and in that branch up to the reunion. The material to build from outside of our families was small, but we had accessions at almost every communion. We had good men on both sides with imperfections, Father Samuel Donnell, prominent in the other branch, and Robert Hamilton and wife in ours.

I felt so miserable when beginning to write that I only intended to acknowledge your invitation. It would be a great pleasure to me to be with you. I trust you will have a better presence, the Holy Spirit, and have a rich baptism. Sincerely yours,

JOHN C. KING.

————

PHILLIPSBURG, KAN., December 13, 1898.

REV. R. A. BARTLETT:

Dear Brother: Your fraternal letter, inviting me to attend the seventy-fifth anniversary of the Kingston (Ind.) church the 18th instant, came duly to hand. It will not be possible for me, on account of distance, to be present at the great meeting anticipated. I have remembered the Kingston church with feelings of great kindness. It was my first charge.

The Concord church was united with it, having half the time. The Kingston church paid $400 and the Concord church $200 of the salary. The Sabbath morning of my first appearance before the church was dark and rainy, April, 1857. The text was Acts 24:25; the sermon was extemporaneous. When I came out of the church, some of the brethren met me in the yard and inquired "What salary would you expect for preaching here and at Concord per year?" My answer was $600. W. W. Hamilton replied, "You shall have it." I spent two years in peace and hard work. The members were of the old, substantial type, faithful and true. The Hamiltons, the Antrobuses, the Grahams, the Donnells, the Hopkinses, the Lowes and the Robisons, all of blessed memory, were at Kingston in my day. Mrs. Adams, who used to live at McCoy's Station, took tea at our house a few years ago at Wamego, Kas., said she remembered me at Kingston, and thought me quite a dude. I took dinner during the meeting of synod at Hutchinson at Dr. Ardery's. His wife was a Reeder, daughter of one of the elders at

Concord. It was pleasant to meet Mr. Reeder after almost forty years of separation from him.

I must soon close this letter. The last mention is that of young Samuel Hamilton. He used to come to church at Kingston very regularly with his little family. I found him an elder in the church at Kingman, Kan. Thomas Lowe, his son-in-law, lived on the farm, about two miles from town. Mr. Samuel Hamilton was an intelligent, Christian gentleman. Mrs. Hamilton was a most excellent Christian woman. I used to stay at their house while I preached at Kingman ; he died while I supplied the church. The attendance at the funeral was very large ; a great procession followed him to the grave. Since that, his dear daughter Jessie went to join him and many loved ones who had entered into rest.

The words of the apostle is my prayer. Heb. 13:20, 21.

Yours truly,   H. M. SHOCKLEY.

KINGMAN, KAN., December 13, 1898.

From the " wild and woolly West " to the Presbyterian church of Kingston, greeting ! You who have never broken loose from old friendships and associations can hardly realize the wave of homesickness which overtakes the wanderer who has strayed beyond the reach of these pleasant gatherings. I think it is such as a child feels when far away from home on Thanksgiving. He knows the festivities are going on in the old homestead, just as in the past. Though we cannot be with you in person, we are there in spirit.

Imagination pictures the whole scene — the kindly, familiar faces, the old pastor, associate and friend for a quarter of a century. How glad I should be to clasp the hands of Mr. and Mrs. Rankin once again, as well as of many others who will be there ! How glad to hear the talks, the songs and the reminiscences ! Last, but not least, to partake of the dinner in the basement, a dinner for which the earth has yielded her richest and best ; and when prepared by cooks of rare skill, will be " a feast fit for the gods." Those big dinners at Kingston have disproved the theory that rich foods impair digestion, produce dyspepsia and all its kindred ills. For have not scores of us made triumphal marches from one big dinner to another? Yet there is not a more healthful people upon the face of the earth, nor a greater number who have reached their allotted time.

As we could not be present to hear the history of the church, we did the next best thing —we took from its place among the treasures left by those who have passed away Father Hamilton's history, written in 1857, and read it aloud to the family. In this day they had no thought of carpets, or frescoing, or basements, but they laid a foundation which I believe will last for many generations. Let us pray that their posterity may build walls not only beautiful, but as lasting as the foundation.

With kindest regards to all, I will say farewell and good-bye.

M. A. HAMILTON.

CONVERSE, IND., December 14, 1898.

TO THE PRESBYTERIAN CHURCH OF KINGSTON, IND.:

My Dear and Much Loved Friends: I have been kindly invited to be with you on this occasion, and regret exceedingly that circumstances are such as to compel me to decline the invitation, with thanks. I can hardly

INTERIOR VIEW OF KINGSTON CHURCH.

think of any visit that would give me more real pleasure than a visit to Kingston at this time and under the present circumstances. I look back to the years spent with you as among the happiest years of my life. I deem it an honor to have been superintendent of your Sunday-school and leader of your choir, and to have been intrusted by you with the honorable and responsible office of an elder. I feel that the years spent with you were profitable ones to me, and trust they were not altogether unprofitable to the church and community. Through your church and him who was then your pastor, I received under God the final impulse which launched me into the gospel ministry, for which I have ever since had occasion to thank God most heartily. So you will believe me when I say that Kingston church has a very warm place in my heart.

And, now, permit me to congratulate you on having reached the seventy-fifth anniversary of your birth as a church. God has spared you to a good old age, and made you a blessing to your community, while He has given you daughters and granddaughters in the other Presbyterian churches of the county. Then you have sent out a goodly number to become identified with other churches, and there help carry on the Master's work. You have also sent forth a number of sons to be preachers of the everlasting Gospel of our Lord Jesus Christ. Some of these have done, and are still doing, grand work for the Master and for the mother church.

Think of the good accomplished by the churches which have grown from yours, and by the workers you have sent out. I cannot give statistics for others, but even your humble servant, the writer, has been permitted, by God's blessing, to welcome some 500 into the fold. Probably others of the brethren have accomplished far more, and, for the thousands blessed and saved through the instrumentality of all these, you will share in the reward. As you think of the good already accomplished, and what is likely to be the final result of the train of influences set in motion by this church, have you not reason to thank and bless God that, seventy-five years ago, he put it into the hearts of the fathers to organize the Sand Creek Presbyterian church? You may well thank Him for His watchful care over it, for the blessings showered upon it, and for the blessings carried from it to others. You have had many noble men and women among you; but, as in fancy I look over the congregation, I miss many, oh, so many, familiar faces of thirty-five or forty years ago, and am constrained to say: "The fathers; where are they?"

Some of the founders of this church had passed away before it was my privilege to know it; but I look in vain for most of the elderly fathers and mothers of thirty-five or forty years ago—the Hamiltons, the Donnells, the McCoys, the Hopkins, and others—who were then the old people. Most of them are gone to the church above. Their mantles have fallen to their children. Are they so wearing them as to honor their parents' church and their parents' God? May God help the present generation to be as faithful, as true, as devoted, as the past; yea, even to surpass the fathers and the mothers in all these things. You are rightly striving to surpass the fathers in arts, science, agriculture, etc.; why not determine, by God's help, to be better, more zealous, more thoroughly consecrated Christians and church-workers than even your fathers and mothers were? Why should not the church and God expect you to accomplish far more than they?

My prayer is that the Lord will help you all to be faithful and successful in doing His work; that this church may grow and prosper more and more, and be a rich source of blessing to all coming generations while time shall last, and that we may, each one, finally hear the loving Master's voice say: "Well done, good and faithful servant; enter into the joy of thy Lord."

Yours fraternally,

GEO. D. PARKER.

---

1 I love Thy kingdom, Lord,
  The house of Thine abode,
  The church our blest Redeemer saved
  With His own precious blood.

2 I love Thy church, O God!
  Her walls before Thee stand,
  Dear as the apple of Thine eye,
  And graven on Thine hand.

3 For her my tears shall fall,
  For her my prayers ascend;
  To her my cares and toils be given,
  Till toils and cares shall end.

4 Beyond my highest joy
  I prize her heavenly ways,
  Her sweet communion, solemn vows,
  Her hymns of love and praise.

5 Sure as Thy truth shall last,
  To Zion shall be given
  The brightest glories earth can yield,
  And brighter bliss of heaven.

KINGSTON PRESBYTERIAN CHURCH.

www.ingramcontent.com/pod-product-compliance
Lightning Source LLC
Chambersburg PA
CBHW031758090426
42739CB00008B/1059